The Art of Tying the BASS FLY

Flies for Largemouth Bass, Smallmouth Bass, and Pan Fish

Skip Morris

Illustrations by
Richard Bunse

DEDICATION

Deflating their accomplishments to fit into a mere page would be an injustice to Dave Whitlock and Lefty Kreh. So I'll just say this: they've more than earned my respect, and it's my honor to dedicate *The Art of Tying the Bass Fly, Second Edition* to them both.

Published by:
Frank Amato Publications, Inc.
PO Box 82112
Portland, Oregon 97282
(503) 653-8108
www.amatobooks.com

Sprial Softbound
ISBN-13: 978-1-57188-484-8
UPC: 0-81127-00326-6

All photographs taken by the author except where noted.

Illustrations: Richard Bunse

Bood Design: Tony Amato

Printed in China

1 3 5 7 9 10 8 6 4 2

CONTENTS

ACKNOWLEDGMENTS

Just as with the original edition of *The Art of Tying the Bass Fly*, this new edition was a group effort. Why? Because I couldn't have picked the right flies to bring the book properly up to date and have gotten those flies and all their details correct without a lot of help from a bunch of sharp tiers and fly fishers. Others contributed too in important ways. So…

My deepest thanks to those who shared with me their water (for my research on the flies in this book), their knowledge, or both. Stan Fagerstrom, whose book *Catch More Bass* was a huge influence on my fishing clear back in the 70s and since, for kindly helping me find some good places to test flies. Stan's friend Maurie Hall for directing me to places where I could find plenty of bluegill to show my new flies. Roger Hudspeth for access to his lake of giant bluegill. Troy Dettman for introducing me to the John Day River and its smallmouth. Bruce Harpole and the Oregon Fishing Club, back when I lived in Portland, for access to their nearby pond to which a new theory or fly pattern was often rushed for testing. Barry Serviente for bringing me out to the Susquehanna River and introducing me to white perch and rock bass. Ed Story, who for so long ran Feather-Craft Fly Fishing so well, for leading me to my first green sunfish. Jim Molitor for the use of his cabin as a headquarters for me to really explore smallmouth bass

on the Umpqua River. To Robbie and Gene for a guided tour of the Susquehana and a few hours on a pond of huge bluegill. To Frank Gibbins for tying Carol into a smallmouth so big her *whoop* was heard a mile down the lake. To Ray Pelland for manning the photographer's boat all afternoon on a largemouth lake while Carol took photos for this book. To Bob Story of Feather-Craft Fly Fishing and Mike Mercer of The Fly Shop for helping me determine which new bass and pan-fish flies have proven themselves and consequently caught on over the past few years. To Steve Kennerk of the Rocky Mountain Dubbing Company for sending me samples of dyed antelope hair and enlightening me as to its uses for making bass flies.

My deepest thanks to those who took the time to help me get their fly patterns, or someone else's, right: Dave Whitlock, Joe Messinger Jr., Chris Helm, Lefty Kreh, Ken Menard, Dan Byford, John Betts, Jack Ellis, Pat Ehlers, Jesse Riding, Brent Hinds, and John Barr.

My deepest thanks to those who helped combine the flies, ideas, and photographs into this concise, efficient, and handsome volume: Tony Amato for his usual tasteful and efficient layout, Carol Ann Morris for her artful photographs and for helping me and Tony search out typos and inconsistencies, and Frank Amato for giving us all the opportunity to pitch in and do this.

FOREWORD

After 65 years of fly fishing, I have come to the conclusion that fly fishing for bass and pan fish is the 'other' half of fresh water fly fishing, and their recent growth in popularity seems to verify my belief. Why has there just recently been so much interest in this other type of fly fishing? I feel there are three main reasons for this. First and most important is that these fish are simply 'lower stress' quarries and more fun to catch. Secondly, they are far more widely distributed and more abundant than trout and their cold water friends. And third, I think it is because bass and pan fish tackle and flies have, over the past 40 years, undergone a major revolution in refinement and are now on an equal basis in quality and design as those used in fly fishing for cold water species of trout, char, grayling and salmon.

Bass and pan fish aggressively feed on a wider range of live foods than cold water fish. Contrary to past popular belief, bass and pan fish are not typically just witless, gullible gluttons, but actually become selective feeders faster than trout. The sunfish family, of which bass are members, has actually been shown to have a higher IQ than the trout family. So, the more closely their natural foods are imitated, the more and larger fish you will catch. Typically, too, these food imitations, compared to cold water flies, average larger in size, are more animate and often require unique materials, shapes, actions, sounds and snag guarding. For instance, a typical, well designed bass fly, because of its larger size, heavier weight, higher air resistance and its unique water action, must be proportioned, balanced and constructed more precisely than the typical trout fly. I've always looked at bass flies as active puppets of live bass foods. Bass and pan fish flies must also be more durable, as they usually encounter more abuse from casting, presentation, animation and fish mauling.

Therefore, it follows that tying bass and pan fish flies successfully calls for truly precise instructions and equally explicit illustrations and photographs. To say the least, authoring a bass and pan fish tying text is a formidable challenge that only a few are skilled enough to accomplish. In my opinion, some of the finest work in publishing fly-tying manuals today is being done by Skip Morris. Skip, with over 45 years of fly-tying and teaching experience and over 40 years background in bass and pan fishing, is well qualified to author this important subject. Skip incorporates in *The Art of Tying the Bass Fly* the classic standards from top to bottom that you should find very useful in order to learn good methods and designs. Skip and I predict that you'll discover, with this book, not only excellent instructions for the best of the current bass and pan fish flies, but also an unlimited source of ideas for designing and tying *new fly puppets!*

This book is truly a good news-worthy addition to our sport, and one that I am pleased and proud to be part of. It is a major contribution to the fun 'other half' of fly fishing and will enrich any fly tier's library and skills. All of us fly tiers and fly fishers owe Skip Morris a bass fly size thanks for his contributions to this sport.

—*Dave Whitlock*

I. ESSENTIAL TECHNIQUES

It would be a peculiar fly pattern indeed whose tying did not require at least a couple of the techniques described here—they're really the foundation of fly tying. If you're so new to tying flies that you don't know them yet, learn them—well. If you already know them, perhaps a review will tighten them up.

ADDING HEAD CEMENT

The finishing knot on a fly (several half hitches or a whip finish) is secured with head cement. There are commercially made head cements, but I prefer epoxy glue, which is very tough. Use a low-vapor epoxy (right now I'm using Devcon 2-Ton Crystal Clear Epoxy) and ventilation.

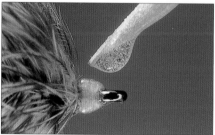

1. Simply add head cement to a thread head or thread-collar with something pointed—a bodkin, toothpick, or the like. Thin cements soak right in; syrupy epoxy glue must be spread out into a layer. Use only a modest amount of cement and try to keep it from filling the hook's eye. If necessary, swab out the eye by pulling a small hackle or body-feather through it.

DUBBING

The word "dubbing" means (1) a fur or synthetic fiber or (2) the act of using such fur or fiber in making fly bodies and heads. It's both a material and a technique. Dubbing is dubbed frequently in trout flies and often enough in pan-fish flies.

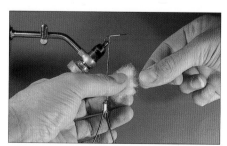

1. Hold your bobbin and a ball of dubbing in your left hand (Right-hander's instructions). Pull a few fibers off the side of the ball with your right hand.

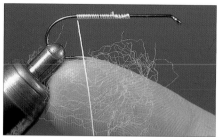

2. Hold the dubbing against the thread with the first finger of your right hand.

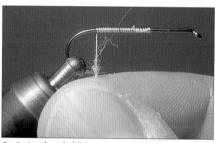

3. Spin the dubbing—in *one* direction *only*—between your thumb and first finger. Keep spinning on dubbing until several inches of thread are layered with it.

4. Wind the dubbing-layered thread up the shank to create a fly-body or head.

HALF HITCH

The fly tier's standard knot for finishing a fly is the whip finish, but three half hitches can do the same work, and the half hitch has other uses. I suggest that once you are comfortable with the half hitch, you tackle the whip finish.

THE HALF HITCH

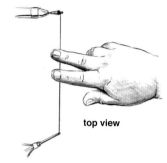

top view

1. Swing your bobbin toward you until the thread is horizontal. Spread the first and second fingers of your right hand (right-hander's instructions) and lay their tips on the thread. Your palm should be down.

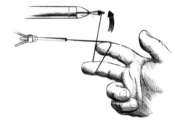

2. Rotate your right wrist until your fingers point up. As you do this, raise your bobbin, and then lower it to your left. The thread should now cross itself in an "X."

3. Catch the far side of the loop over the hook or fly.

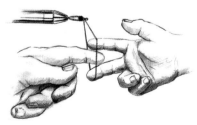

4. Let your bobbin hang. Take the loop from your right-hand fingers with the first finger of your left hand.

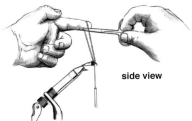

side view

5. Use something smooth and pointed—closed scissor blades, a bobbin, a hatpin—to take the loop from your finger.

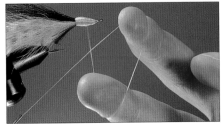

6. Pull down on your bobbin as you guide the half-hitch loop closed.

1. Create a half-hitch loop and slip it over the thread-collar or thread-head.

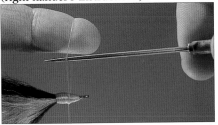

2. Pass the loop from your two right-hand fingers to the first finger of your left hand (right-hander's instructions).

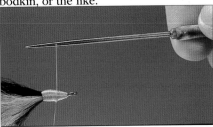

3. Take the loop from your finger with something smooth and pointed—the closed blades of your scissors, a hatpin, a bodkin, or the like.

4. Pull your bobbin down as you guide the loop closed with the pointed object.

Light Turn

The light-tension thread-turn, which I simply call the "light turn," is used to bind relatively stiff materials to a hook.

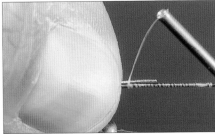

1. Hold the material atop the hook's shank, take a light-tension turn of thread around material and shank, and then pull that turn tight. The trick is to use just enough tension to control the thread but not so much tension that the material is pushed around the shank.

Pinch

The "pinch" is a technique for binding a soft material atop a hook's shank.

THE PINCH

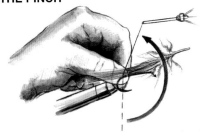

1. Hold the material atop the hook's shank. Swing your bobbin to your right and up (right-hander's instructions).

2. Move the joints of your left-hand thumb and first finger closer together. This will spread the very tips of your thumb and finger. Tug the thread back between your *thumb* and the material.

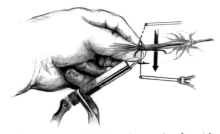

3. Lower your bobbin down the far side of the hook, and then tug the thread back between your *fingertip* and the material.

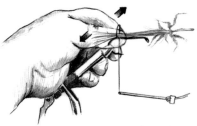

4. Widen the gap between the joints of your left-hand thumb and first finger, so the tips roll forward. Now the shank, material, and a loop of thread are locked firmly between your thumb and finger.

5. Pull down on your bobbin until the thread loop is tightly closed. Pull the bobbin towards you a bit.

6. The material should now be secured atop the shank. Add a few tight thread-turns in the same place immediately, before a moment's slack can undo what you've accomplished.

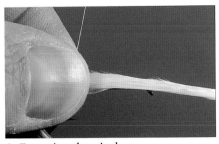

1. Executing the pinch.

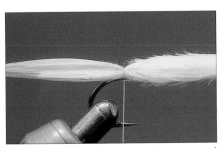

2. The results of a properly executed pinch.

Starting Thread

Starting the thread is easy, and absolutely essential to tying a fly.

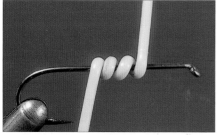

1. Hold the end of the thread down against the hook's shank. Wind the thread forward (towards the hook's eye) in a few tight turns. (Fly line is shown here in place of thread, for clarity).

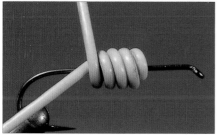

2. Wind the thread back (towards the hook's bend) in a few tight turns over the first turns. The thread is now locked on. Trim its end and tie the fly.

The Triangle

The "triangle" is my method of drawing back materials from a hook's eye, for ease in building a thread head, but you will discover other uses for it.

1. Bring the tips of your left-hand first finger, second finger, and thumb lightly together. The result is the roughly triangular opening you see here in the center. (Right-hander's instructions.)

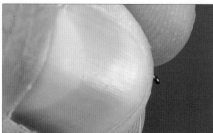

2. Cup your left hand over the fly and draw the triangle's opening back over the hook's eye.

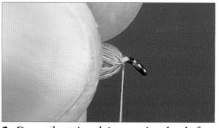

3. Draw the triangle's opening back further, allowing the thread to slip through as you do so (keeping the thread taut helps). Now you should have clear access for building a thread-head.

Whip Finish

Intimidation has kept many a tier from learning the whip finish. It shouldn't—the whip finish is really only a half hitch that forgot to stop. And it's the standard fly tier's finishing knot.

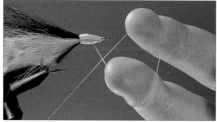

1. Start the whip finish as you would a half hitch by slipping the thread-loop over the hook.

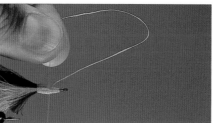

2. I call the near side of the thread-loop the "working-side" and the far side the "passive-side." Lift the working-side up and then hold it there firmly; release the passive-side. Let the bobbin hang.

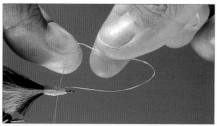

3. Pass the working-side from hand to hand as you wind it forward in three or more turns. Keep tension on the working side, and make certain the passive-side stays out in front of the hook's eye. With the passive-side out in front, you are winding over it with the working-side; if you are not winding over the passive-side, then you are accomplishing nothing.

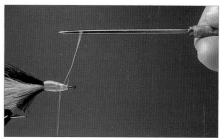

4. Close the thread-loop as usual.

THE WHIP FINISH

1. Proceed as you would for a half hitch by slipping the thread-loop over the hook. I call the near side of the loop the "working-side" and the far side of the loop the "passive-side."

2. Let your bobbin hang. Bring the passive-side of the loop forward and keep it there as you wind the working-side forward in three or more turns.

II. SNAG GUARDS

If you cast your flies around sunken logs and brush and back into patches of lily pads and other water plants—which smallmouth-bass anglers sometimes do and largemouth-bass anglers regularly do—you'll want snag guards on those flies. A snag guard does exactly what its name implies—it protects a fly from hooking things other than bass.

There are two basic forms of the snag guard. The "single-loop snag guard" (my name for it) is just a loop of monofilament running from the hook's bend to its eye. It's really the standard. The "double-loop snag guard" (again, my name) has crept into some popularity. It's made of two loops of monofilament.

I generally use 3/0 thread for binding on my snag guards, but some tiers prefer flat waxed nylon or even heavier threads (see "Threads" in section X, "Bass-Fly Materials").

Jack Ellis was the first (as far as I know) to add a snag guard to a pan-fish fly. I'd always assumed pan-fish flies were too light and small and pan-fish's takes were too gentle for a snag-guard to work on a pan-fish fly. Jack proved me wrong. You can find out more about the pan-fish snag guard in "The Fathead Diver" in section IX, "Pan-Fish Flies."

THE SINGLE-LOOP SNAG GUARD

Here's the old reliable. It's normally tied with a hard, stiff monofilament leader called Mason, in 20-pound test. I've always preferred my snag guards light, for fear of missing hard-won strikes on the heavier stuff. I use Mason as light as 12-pound test on my smallest bass flies and up to 15 on big ones. When I tell experienced bass fly fishers that I'm leery of the 20-pound, they tell me that they use it all the time and rarely miss a fish. I think I'm cautious, they think I'm neurotic. Perhaps I'm a cautious neurotic and we're both right.

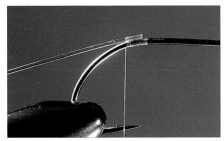

1. Start some 3/0 thread near the bend. Bind one end of the monofilament atop the shank at the bend, with tight thread-turns.

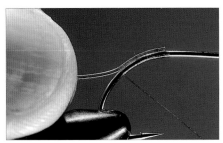

2. Begin wrapping close, tight thread-turns down the bend and mono. Hold the mono back under light tension, to keep it atop the shank. Most tiers wind thread about one third down the bend. Some tiers continue to halfway of the bend or even further. Remember: the further you wrap, the better the completed snag guard will stay properly aligned, but also the stiffer it will become. Personal choice. Experiment.

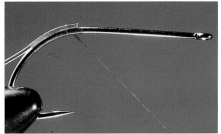

3. Wrap the thread back up the shank and mono in close, tight turns. This part of the snag guard is complete.

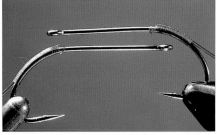

4. Here's a snag guard wrapped one third down the bend and another beyond halfway.

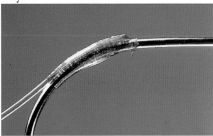

5. Some tiers coat the snag-guard windings with head-cement and let them set overnight before continuing. They'll wrap and coat several snag guards in one session. The snag guard shown here is coated with epoxy glue. The point is to toughen the thread-wraps, but I've never had a problem with the durability of uncoated snag-guard windings. Another approach is to use tougher thread—flat waxed nylon, rod-winding thread, whatever.

6. Use the same 3/0 thread to bind on the tail, whatever tail the pattern dictates. You may have to switch threads after completing the tail if your next step is flaring hair—this, of course, depends on which thread you used for the snag guard and tail. Complete the tying of the fly.

7. Lock the fly in the jaws of your vise with the mono *inside* the jaws behind the hook's bend, as shown. Restart the 3/0 thread at the hook's eye (of course if the whole fly was tied with the 3/0, there's no need to restart it; just continue with the 3/0 from beginning to end).

8. Bring the mono up through the hook's eye. Secure it there with a few snug (not tight) thread-turns. Now the mono should be bound *beneath* the shank only. Adjust the snag-guard loop to size; then add a few tight thread-turns.

9. Push and pinch the end of the mono back hard, until it takes a set.

10. Add tight thread-turns over the mono. You are now winding thread around the mono both above and below the shank.

11. Lift the end of the mono and trim it closely. Use fingernail clippers or cut deep inside your scissors' blades—not with the points. Whip finish the thread and trim it. Add some head cement to the thread-turns and the single-loop snag guard is complete.

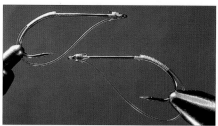

12. How large should the snag-guard loop be? It must at least be large enough to guard the hook's point. Some tiers make the loop big, well out from the point; others make it smaller, almost touching the point. The bigger the loop, the better it resists snags—and fish. But that's relative to how hard you set the hook and how snaggy the water is that you fish. The photograph shows a very small loop and a big one. Most snag-guard loops will fall somewhere in between these two extremes. Experiment.

THE DOUBLE-LOOP SNAG GUARD

Theoretically, the double-loop snag guard provides more snag protection than the single-loop, but opinions vary.

Even though you'd expect to use mono only half as heavy for a double-loop guard as for a single-loop, most tiers use the same 20-pound Mason for all their snag guards despite this logic and have no complaints.

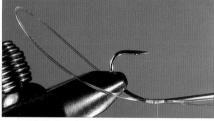

1. Lock a hook, inverted, into your vise. Start some 3/0 thread at the hook's bend. Double some snag-guard monofilament into a loop. Bind the ends of the loop onto the sides of the shank, at the bend. (Some tiers find it easiest to bind the ends of the loop on one at a time.) The loop should lie back over the jaws of your vise. You can position the ends of the mono to the sides of the hook's shank by pressing down on them with your thumbnail.

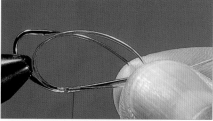

2. Bend the loop forward and hook it over the hook's eye; then pinch the sides of the loop together. Now you can see if the loop needs adjusting (this one is too small).

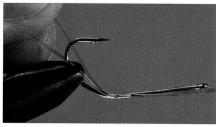

3. Pull on the loop, or its ends, to adjust the loop's size. Check the loop at the hook's eye again. Keep adjusting and checking until the loop is the right size.

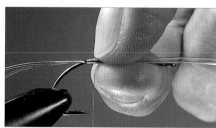

4. Remove the hook from your vise, turn the hook over, and remount it in the normal upright position in your vise. Add tight thread-turns around the mono at the bend and just up from the bend, usually forward to directly over the hook's point. Press down on the ends of the mono with your thumbnail now and then as you add the turns; this pressing keeps the mono down on the sides of the hook's shank.

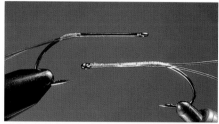

5. Dave Whitlock sometimes winds thread over the mono's ends right up the shank, then gives the windings a coating of Zap-A-Gap. This creates a flat thread-base for flared hair. One of the snag guards shown here was formed in Dave's style; the other's mono-ends were cut closely, conventionally.

6. Use the snag-guard thread to bind on the tail; then complete the tying of the fly (with whatever thread is appropriate). Start the 3/0 thread again at the hook's eye.

7. Remove the fly from your vise, bend the mono-loop forward, and return the hook to your vise. Raise your bobbin straight up over the hook's eye. Hook the mono-loop over the eye, and then make a couple of tight thread-turns in front of the mono-loop. Now there is at least one tight turn of thread holding the mono in place.

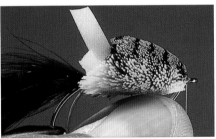

8. Bring your left hand (right-hander's instructions) up under the jaws of your vise and pull the mono loop down as you pinch its sides tightly together. Pinch the mono up close to the hook's eye, but just far enough away from the eye to allow you to add thread-turns over the mono. Add lots of tight thread-turns over the mono and shank, whip finish and trim the thread, and then add a tough cement—I use epoxy—all over the thread-turns.

9. The completed double-loop guard. If you want the sides of the mono-loop closer together, pinch the end of the loop with pliers before binding it. Also, the further back over the mono you wrap the thread, the closer together the mono-loops will end up.

THE SNAG GUARD AS A CHECK

It's nearly impossible for hair that's tightly flared to slide back past the end of a mono snag guard. So I often use a snag guard as a check, to keep flared hair (and perhaps a tail) from slipping down the bend as it's being compressed back. I usually use this approach when flaring hair on a bare shank, rather than on a base of tight thread-turns. The single-loop snag guard works better as a check than the double-loop.

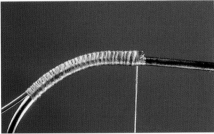

1. Using 3/0 thread (or whatever thread you use for your snag guards), tightly bind the end of the snag-guard monofilament at the point on the hook's shank where you will start flaring hair. Bind the mono down the hook's bend, as usual.

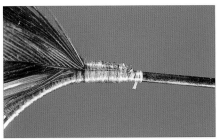

2. Bind on the tail, if there is one, at the bend, over or along the sides of the mono. Advance the 3/0 thread to just ahead of the end of the mono. Whip finish and trim the thread.

3. Start the hair-flaring thread over the whip finish in the 3/0 thread. It is critical that the hair-flaring thread starts *in front of the mono*.

4. Begin flaring hair in the normal fashion. As you compress the hair back, it will travel no further than the bound end of the mono.

III. Flaring and Shaping Hair

If you don't know how to flare and compress deer hair and trim it, you won't get far with tying bass flies—bass flies are, more than anything else, about flared hair. In fact, there are probably more flared-hair fly dressings for bass than for all other fishes combined.

Hair for flaring is filled with air pockets, making it light and very buoyant, and sort of spongy feeling when you squeeze it. Because of this sponginess the hair bristles when tightly bound—and it's that bristling, or flaring, that makes so many fascinating fly designs possible.

The standard hair for flaring is deer, the next most common is elk, and most bass-fly tiers don't even know about antelope hair but might like it if they try it. Regardless of which type of hair you flare, it should be thick-shafted and spongy. For more about these and other pocketed hairs, see "Hairs for Flaring" in section X, "Bass-Fly Materials." There are several good threads for flaring hair, and these too are discussed in section X. For now, just use white or gray size-A rod-winding thread, the dependable standard.

There are also several threads for binding on a snag guard and tail (see section II, "Snag Guards" and "Hackle Tail" in section IV), but just use 3/0 for now. When the tail is complete, whip finish the 3/0 in front of the tail's butts, start the rod-thread over the 3/0, trim off the 3/0 and the tag-end of the rod-thread, and then begin flaring hair.

Spinning Hair

There are many ways to spin hair on a hook. The problem is that most of them are lousy ways—they'll fail you half the time and you'll groan when you see the results. Spinning hair made a wreck of me until—finally!—I figured out how to make it work consistently, cleanly, and easily.

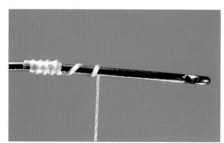

1. With the rod-thread started, advance it in two or three open spirals up the bare shank.

2. Snip off a bunch of hair close to the hide. The bunch should be about the diameter of a pencil. Hold the hair bunch near its tips and comb out the underfur and short hairs. Nearly any type of comb will do; only combs with very close teeth will pose problems.

3. Trim off the tips of the hairs.

4. Hold the hair-bunch to the shank as shown: between your left-hand thumb and fingers (right-hander's instructions, of course), on the near side of the shank, the top of the bunch tipping back, bottom of the bunch tipping forward. (It doesn't matter whether the butts are up or down.) Take *three* turns of thread around the hair bunch and shank. The turns should be of light tension, halfway between the butts and trimmed tips of the hair.

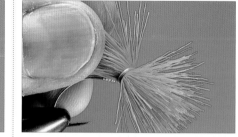

5. Pull slowly down on the thread until the turns tighten just *slightly*. As you continue to gradually tighten the thread, the bunch will start to flare and want to spin around the shank. As soon as the bunch flares even a *little*, start releasing the ends of the hairs a few at a time. Continue steadily tightening the thread and releasing more and more hair-ends as the bunch twists around the shank.

Notice that the hair-ends are springing free from my grasp—that's important. Don't just loosen your grip on the bunch—let the ends of the hairs spring completely free.

6. Release any remaining hair-ends as you pull hard on the thread; the hair should spin once or even twice around the shank. If you have properly balanced the releasing of the hairs with the tightening of the thread, the hairs should now be evenly distributed around the shank. (This proper balance takes some practice, so don't be easily discouraged.)

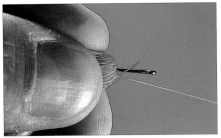

7. Draw all the hair back with your thumb, first finger, and second finger. You can stroke the hair back a few times if needed. With the hair now drawn back, pull the thread down tight. Keep the thread tight, not allowing even a moment of slack from now until it is locked firmly in place by a few tight turns or a half hitch. Pull the bobbin and thread straight forward—firmly.

8. Wind five tight thread-turns against the front of the spun hair; this locks the hair and thread firmly in place. You can now let the bobbin hang. Another method of securing the thread, which I got from Chris Helm, is to wind on a couple of tight turns in front of the hair and then add a half hitch. I use a half-hitch tool; it allows me to add the hitch without letting slack into the thread.

9. Spin another hair bunch onto the shank as you did the first. After spinning the first hair bunch it is sometimes easiest to hold additional bunches in your right hand and work the three thread-turns on with your left. Be careful not to catch up any hairs from the last bunch in these turns. Hold the hair with your left hand, as usual, to spin it.

10. Each new bunch of spun hair must be tightly compressed back into the last bunch. To do this, support the hair by grasping the shank from behind, tight against the back of the first bunch of hair, and then push the hair back from the front with your thumb and first finger.

The real point here isn't to push the hair back, but to push the *thread* back—get the thread that holds the hair compressed together and the hair will have to follow.

11. This compressing can also be done with a tool called a "hair compressor" or "hair compactor." The hair compressor shown here is called a Brassie.

12. All that flared hair at the hook's eye makes a whip finish very difficult to execute. Here's where the half-hitch tool becomes indispensible—with it you can easily slip three half hitches in past all those hairs without catching any. Trim the thread closely. The next step is to shape the flared hair.

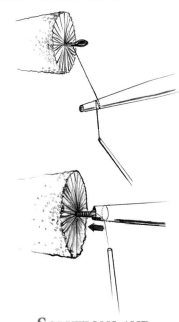

SOLUTIONS AND SUGGESTIONS FOR SPINNING AND COMPRESSING HAIR

1. Most of the instructions I've seen for spinning hair suggest two turns of thread around the bunch. But I add *three* turns to insure that the spinning hair won't fly off the hook.

2. Since I can't say it enough, I'll say it again: *it's the balance between the tightening of the thread and the release of the hair that makes hair spin.*

3. Make sure you start releasing hairs *as soon* as the hair begins to flare even a little. Waiting too long to release hairs will kill your chances of spinning hair.

4. Though redundancy can be a writer's plague, this (like #2) is simply too important to say only once, so: as you release the hairs, their tips must spring *completely free* of your grasp. Just loosening your grasp on the hairs isn't enough.

5. It's the distribution of the hair that allows the bunch to really spin. Think of the rounded hair-shafts as the steel balls in a ball bearing—if the steel balls are all on one side, there is too much friction; but if they are distributed around the inner housing and separate it from the outer, everything spins freely.

Again, it's the proper balance of thread tightening and hair release—with the hair-tips released completely—that distributes the hairs around the shank and allows the spinning. Yes, that's the third time I've said this; obviously teaching fly tying has made me an expert at repetition and a master of redundancy.

6. Because you want the hair secured tightly, maintain firm, constant tension on the thread after you draw back the spun hair and pull the thread tight. Even a moment's slack will leave everything loose.

7. During any part of the hair-spinning or hair-compressing process, feel free to grasp the hook and support it in whatever way you see fit. Even heavy wire hooks can flex quite a bit under the stresses of spinning and compressing hair; supporting the hook helps you stay in control.

8. Here's a point you'd probably soon figure out on your own, but perhaps by offering it now I can save you a few perforations—watch out for the hook's point as you compress back each spun-hair bunch. Applying pressure to a hook can get you impaled if you're not careful.

9. Again, to effectively compress hair, you must actually compress the *thread*. If you simply push the hairs together, they'll gradually spread back out, but if you push the securing thread-turns close together you force the hairs to stay compressed.

SPINNING HAIR ON A THREAD BASE

Many experienced bass-fly tiers prefer to spin hair on a tight layer of thread, feeling that this thread-base gives the hair something textured to grip. A sound approach, although I use epoxy glue to lock on the hair instead (as described under the next heading).

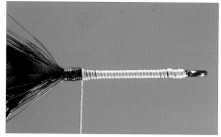

1. There are several ways to make a thread base and spin hair over it, but the way that follows is as sound and as close to standard as any. Bind the tail and snag-guard mono with 3/0 thread. Whip finish the thread in front of the tail. Start the hair-flaring thread at the eye and wind it tightly down the shank to the tail. Cover the whip finish in the 3/0 thread's with windings of heavy hair-flaring thread.

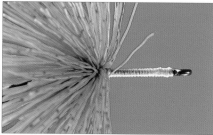

2. Spin and compress hair up the shank to the hook's eye as usual. Yes, you *can* spin and compress hair on a thread base; it's just trickier than on a bare shank.

FLARING HAIR— MY METHOD

Spinning hair is fun and effective, but I seldom do it now. I'll show you the method I find easier than spinning, and it's consistently given me cleaner results.

1. Cut a bunch of hair and comb it. (I don't trim the tips of the hair. No need to.) Hold the hair *atop* the shank.

2. Work the hair down around the shank; basically, this just means pushing it down a bit. For right-handers, hold the hair in your right hand. (In the left hand for left-handers.)

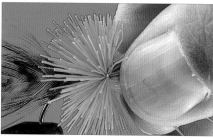

3. Again for right-handers, work the bobbin around the hook with your left hand, adding two turns of thread around the hair. Continue holding the hair firmly in your right hand as you pull the thread down tight. Pull the bobbin toward you, then away from you back and forth as you tighten the thread.

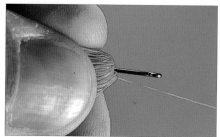

4. Draw back the hair's tips, pull the thread tightly forward, and add five tight thread-turns (or two turns and a half hitch) in front of the flared hair.

5. Flaring is complete for this bunch. Continue flaring and compressing hair to the hook's eye.

6. I usually add epoxy to the shank before flaring a bunch of hair with my method—if I'm flaring on bare shank. Makes the fly tough. But avoid getting epoxy on your hands or fingers. Not healthy.

STACKING HAIR COLORS

Stacking hair colors results in flies of one color below the shank and another, or even several others, above. The most common and logical approach is to create a pale belly and dark back, like real frogs and mice and fishes. But bass flies don't always and needn't always resemble real creatures.

The method I'll demonstrate here is my own. I like to leave the hair's tips untrimmed, which makes stacking hair colors easier. You'll see why soon.

1. Cut and comb a bunch of belly hair, about half the amount you'd use for spinning. Don't trim the tips of the hair. Secure the hair lightly atop the shank with two turns of thread; the hair's tips should be forward, projecting over and beyond the hook's eye.

2. Use the tight thread to push, to rotate, the belly hair to the underside of the shank.

3. With the belly hair under the shank, push your thumb tip or fingertip straight down firmly onto the shank and hair. Pull the thread down tight. (I like to push up on the hook's eye as I tighten the thread, to support the hook, keep it from bending.) You can now release the bobbin and quit pushing down on the hair and shank. The belly hair should now be firmly locked on below the shank.

4. Cut and comb the top hair (but don't trim its tips). For a single-color back, use the same amount of hair you used for the belly. For a back of more than one color, use *less* back hair than belly hair. Just remember that, in the end, *all* the back hair combined should equal the amount of belly hair. Bind the back hair *lightly* atop the shank and belly hair with two thread-turns. The turns should lie atop the previous two turns securing the belly hair. The tips of the back hair should project back. Work the thread through the white hair carefully, trying not to catch up any hair-tips.

5. Pinch the hair at the sides (some tiers prefer to pinch the hair top and bottom), and then pull the thread downward until it's tight.

6. If you want to add another hair color, mash down the back hair.

7. Cut and comb the next color of hair and bind it lightly atop the back hair with two turns of thread over the previous turns. Try not to catch up any hair-tips.

8. Hold the hair at the sides and pull the thread tight, as before. You can add up to four or five colors in this manner, but remember—you are adding more thread-turns with each color, and those turns can mess up the belly hair.

9. Pull the front ends of the belly-hair down. Because the belly-hair is long and the back-hair is short, it will be easy to separate them.

10. Pull the front ends of the back-hair up and back. If there are a few belly hairs up with the back hair, or vice versa, simply snip out these uncooperative hairs.

Now try to get all the hair pulled tightly back as you pull down hard on the bobbin. Secure the thread as you did with spun hair (a few tight turns or a half hitch).

11. This is what the stacked colors look like when flaring is completed. You could have added even more colors in the back—just so long as the amount of back hair generally equals the amount of belly hair.

12. Compress each new bunch of stacked hair back into the last. Continue stacking hair in this manner to the eye.

SPOTS AND STRIPES

Whenever you add a second hair-bunch of a new color over the top-hair, that second hair-bunch will create either a spot or a stripe, depending on how it's handled.

1. Note that the small bunch of black hair is closely gathered. When the thread is tightened and all the hair is later trimmed, the black will appear as a spot or oval.

2. Here is a Dave's Hare Waterpup. The olive hair-bunch atop its head was kept gathered; the result is this olive oval on the black head.

3. Compare this photo with photo #1 and you'll see that this black hair is spread out in a layer.

4. Here's a close-up of the spread black hair. It can be spread by pushing it down the sides with thumb tip and fingertip, by teasing it with a bodkin, or in any other manner that does the job.

5. With the hair spread over the back hair and held in place, simply pull the thread tight and complete the bunch as usual; then compress it back as usual. Continue stacking, flaring, and compressing hair in this manner up the shank.

6. When all the hair is then trimmed, the hair that was spread over the top will appear as stripes, as it does on this Skip's Fusion Bug.

TRIMMING FLARED HAIR

1. The sharpest razor blade I know of is the double-edge blade (on the left); the single-edge blade (on the right) seems only slightly sharper than a stone axe when I try to cut flared hair with it, which is probably why it is also called a "safety razor." Deer hair is certainly safe around it.

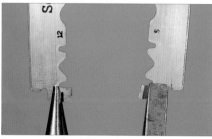

2. You can handle a double-edged blade with less risk if that blade is halved. To halve a blade, hold one side in pliers and cut the blade up the center with tin snips, or use two pairs of pliers, hold each side of the blade with a pair, and then bend the blade back and forth until it breaks at one end, and then break the other end. Always handle razor blades with great care—they are extremely sharp and, in the span of a thought, can cut you deeply.

3. If there are rubber-strand legs in your flared-hair fly, pull them tightly up.

4. Spin the rubber strands tightly together atop the hair and hold them there. Hold the fly by the rubber strands and the top of the hair. If there are no rubber-strand legs, most tiers hold the fly by the hook's bend.

5. Turn the hook so that you are looking straight down the shank from the hook's eye (even though you won't actually see the shank, just the eye and a lot of hair). Make the first cut along the underside of the hair. Even if you plan to trim the underside closely, cut well away from the shank for now—this first cut will let you see the hook's bend and, from that, align the hair's shape with the hook. I prefer to use a razor blade and cut straight back through the hair; a sawing motion can help. Scissors can make the same cut with a few snips.

6. Point the fly straight up so that you are looking at its underside. Make a cut along each side. This will define the general width and shape of the body. Again, the cuts can be made with razor blade or scissors. The curved-blade scissors shown here are handy for shaping some flies, such as this Dave's Diving Frog.

7. Pull the rubber strands firmly *down*, gather them together, and then hold the fly by the strands and the hook's bend.

8. Make a cut along the top—again, to define the hair's shape. You can make the top cut with either scissors or razor blade.

9. Pull the rubber-strands up again and then give the underside of the hair its final trimming. In most cases, you would then round out the body with shallow length-wise strokes of the blade or with shallow snips of the scissors. Remember to keep pulling the rubber-strands up or down to keep them safely away from the cutting.

10. Sometimes it helps to work the blade sideways across the hair, side to side, to round it out.

11. Trim those odd little corners and edges now or any time from now on.

12. If there's a collar of hair-ends, shape it now with scissors. (See "The Dahlberg Diver" for more on shaping hair-collars.) My rule is: the further you are cutting from the shank, the worse a blade works and the better scissors work. You really need both razor blade *and* scissors to shape flared hair.

SOLUTIONS AND SUGGESTIONS FOR TRIMMING FLARED HAIR

1. Don't get fanatical about trimming close to the shank along the fly's underside—if you cut the thread, you'll have to clean the hook off back to the tail and start the hair-flaring all over. Be careful, and watch for the thread as you trim underneath.

2. The side and top cuts should be made with proportion in mind. If these cuts are correct, the finished fly will have good proportions.

3. Avoid touching the razor blade's cutting edge to the hook—the hook's hard steel will easily nick or dull a blade's fine edge.

4. A razor blade's cutting edge won't last long in shaping flared hair. Be prepared to replace a blade if it seems dull.

IV. MORE TECHNIQUES

EYES, BARBELL, BINDING ON

"Barbell eyes" are essentially a ball or some other sort of bulge at each end of a stem, and are usually formed of lead or a lead-substitute or plastic. All barbell eyes can suggest real insect or fish eyes. The lead or lead-substitute ones also add serious weight to a fly.

The method shown here for binding barbell eyes to a hook also applies to bead-chain eyes. (See "Lead" and "Various Materials" in section X, "Bass-Fly Materials.")

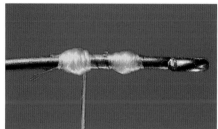

1. Where you'll mount the eyes on the hook's shank, build two balls of tight thread-turns with a gap between them. This step is optional, but it can help you control the position of the eyes. I used single-strand floss as thread here because the floss is thick and easy to see in the photographs.

2. Bind the eyes to the shank with a few modestly tight thread-turns around the hook's shank and the eyes' stem. If you built up the two thread-balls, the eyes' stem should settle between them. You are now seeing the hook and eyes from an oblique angle, somewhere between a top-view and a side-view.

3. Rotate the eye-rounds out to the sides, and then add tight thread-turns crossing the shank and stem from the other direction. Continue alternating the thread from one direction to the other to add tight crisscrossing thread-turns around shank and stem.

4. Occasionally grasp the eyes firmly between your thumb and first finger as you pull the thread very tight. When you feel that the eyes are secure, go on with tying the rest of the fly.

BINDING ON BARBELL EYES

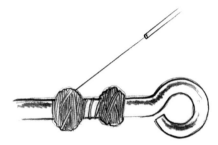

The two balls of thread.

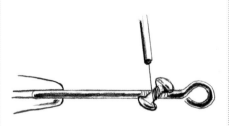

Binding the eyes on with thread-turns in one direction.

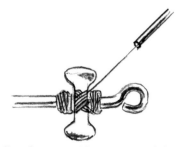

Binding the eyes with crisscrossed thread-turns.

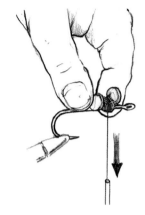

Holding the eyes while pulling the thread tight.

EYES, HOLLOW OR SOLID-PLASTIC, GLUEING ON

Glueing hollow or solid eyes onto flared hair is common practice in tying bass flies. With shaped wool, eyes must be attached to the *shank* (see, "Eyes, Barbell, Binding on" above).

TRIMMING OUT EYE-SOCKETS

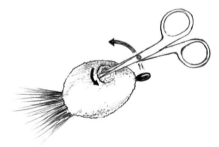

1. When the shaping of the flared hair is complete, trim out sockets for the eyes with scissors. I find it easiest to make lots of tiny snips, slowly widening a socket to proper depth and width. (Some tiers prefer to burn sockets into the hair using a wood-burning tool or the like. If you do this, be certain to scrape out the ash before adding the glue. Personally, I'm not fond of the smell of burnt deer hair.)

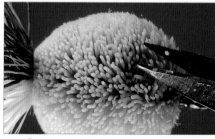

1. I find it easiest to trim across the eye-socket, so that my scissors are cutting at the far side of the socket.

2. This is a completed socket, about the diameter of the eye and not too deep. Trim a socket into each side of the head or body.

3. Work some glue into the socket and hair with a toothpick. I prefer gooey epoxy glue partially cured, but many tiers use a plastic cement, such as Duco, or an all-purpose sealer-glue called Goop.

4. Smear some glue on the back of the eye (some tiers consider this unnecessary).

5. Press the eye into the socket. Prepare the other eye and then press it into the other socket.

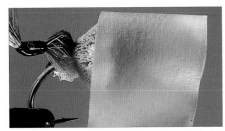

6. If the eyes keep creeping out of the sockets, wrap some 1/2-inch-wide masking tape lightly around them and the hair, and then press the tape ends together underneath. The tape needn't be tight. The next day, cut the tape and peel it off; the eyes will be firmly mounted.

HACKLE TAIL

There's not much to a hackle tail—a few hackles divided into two sets, the sets curving apart (standard on floating bass flies and divers) or cupping together (sometimes on sinking flies). There are two basic approaches to binding on these hackle-sets, and we'll explore them here. Choosing one approach or the other is usually a matter of preference rather than function. There are also several types of hackles that can be used in a hackle tail; these hackle types are explored in section X, "Bass-Fly Materials."

1. Whatever goes inside the tail (such as the snag guard, if you're adding one) must be bound to the shank first. The hackles are divided into two sets (each set with curves matched and tips even). Then both hackle-sets are cut at their base to a single length. The sets shown in this photograph contain two hackles each.

2. To execute the first approach, in which the hackles are bound to the *sides* of the shank, cut the butts of the hackles off but do not strip any fibers from the stems. Simply hold one hackle-set flat against the near side of the shank (usually at the bend) and then add a layer of light-tension thread-turns. The hackles should curve towards you or away, depending on the fly pattern. I normally use 3/0 thread for this work, but I used flat waxed nylon here both because it's a good alternative and because it's thick and therefore shows up well in the photographs.

3. Add a second layer of thread-turns—this layer should be moderately tight. Finally, add the third and final layer—these turns should be tight indeed. Now bind the other hackle-set to the other side of the shank with this same three-layer approach.

If you had simply bound the hackles with one layer of tight thread-turns, the thread's torque would probably have twisted the hackles out of position. The light-tension thread-turns provide a pad against thread-torque when the final tight layer of thread is added.

4. To execute the second approach, in which the hackles are bound *atop* the shank, cut off the butts of the hackles and strip the fibers from the first 1/8 inch or so along the *underside* of the stem only.

5. Holding both hackle sets together, lower their butts to the hook's shank. Add a layer of light-tension thread-turns over the hackles' butts; then a second layer of thread, tighter this time; and finally, a third layer that is tight indeed.

6. Regardless of whether you bound the hackles to the sides or the top of the hook, twist and bend each hackle-set up or out at its base, as needed, to adjust it to the angle you prefer. Normally, each set should be straight back, or tipped slightly up, and vertical along its flats.

RUBBER-STRAND LEGS

There are many ways to add rubber-strand legs to a bass fly, and generally, those ways are straightforward. But adding strand-legs to bass flies of flared hair is another matter, which is why I'll demonstrate it here.

1. Cut the rubber-strands slightly long. Holding all the strands together, ends somewhat evened, make a loose overhand knot at their center—one knot containing all the strands. Slip the knot over the hook's eye and down the shank to the front of the flared hair; the knot itself should be atop the shank. This photograph shows knotted strands in place on the hook and another set of strands that are knotted and ready for the next fly.

2. Pull the ends of the strands firmly, to close and tighten the knot.

ADDING RUBBER-STRAND LEGS

1. Make a loose overhand knot in the strands.

2. Slip the knot down the hook's shank and pull the knot tight.

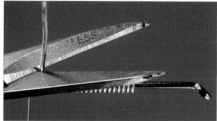

3. Jimmy Nix binds the strand-knot with tight crisscrossed turns of thread. Chris Helm simply works the thread to the front of the strands in one spiraled half-turn, and relies on the compression of the following hair-bunches to lock the strand-knot in place. In either case, the thread should wind up in front of the strand-knot in a few tight turns or a half hitch. Compress the knot back into the flared hair, and then continue flaring and compressing hair. (See section III, "Flaring and Shaping Hair" for help in shaping the hair without cutting the rubber-strands.)

LEAD

A lot of sinking bass and pan-fish flies are weighted with lead (or lead-substitute) wire wrapped on the hook's shank. Adding lead to a hook is easy enough, but if it is added incorrectly, the lead-turns become a flimsy foundation over which to tie the fly and make that tying difficult. (Some flies are weighted with lead bar-bell or bead-chain eyes, but that's another matter, dealt with in this section under "Eyes, Barbell, Binding on.")

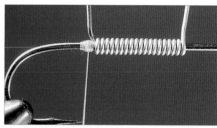

1. With the thread started near the bend, wrap a layer of lead wire tightly up the shank in close turns. (It's much easier to create a flared-hair head on bare shank than on lead, so if there is to be such a head, end the lead-wraps short of it.)

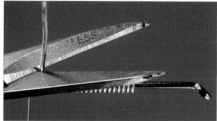

2. Some lead and lead-substitute wire is soft enough that you can hold the hook and pull the wire until it breaks at the hook's shank. Some wire is too strong for pulling; if so, cut the wire closely deep inside your scissors' blades or with the tips of old scissors or with fingernail clippers. If the ends of the lead stick out, press them down with your thumbnail or the closed blades of your scissors.

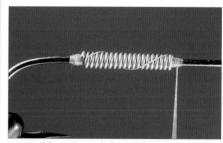

3. Build a thread-dam of tight turns at the rear of the lead; then spiral the thread sharply forward to the front of the lead wraps and build a thread-dam there. The lead is now secured; continue tying the fly.

Skip's Whip

The Skip's whip is a whip finish with head cement all through it. I use it often for foam-flies, especially those in which the final whip finish is sunken into a crease of foam—only the Skip's whip can easily and neatly carry head cement down that crease to the thread. But the Skip's whip has lots of other applications—most flies that lack a full thread-head are candidates for a Skip's Whip.

1. Add head cement or epoxy glue sparingly along 1/4 inch to 1/2 inch of the thread, close to the hook. (Use ventilation or work outdoors and try to find epoxy or head cement with minimal vapors.)

2. Add one to three thread-turns at the whip-finish site.

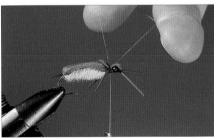

3. Make a whip finish as usual, but don't get the head cement or epoxy on your fingers. Working with a large thread-loop can help you accomplish this.

4. Guide the thread-loop closed with something smooth and pointed—a bodkin or hatpin or the like. This keeps you from getting the cement or epoxy on your fingers. Trim the thread closely. The Skip's whip is complete. The end of the thread hanging from the bobbin will be wet with cement or epoxy; trim it off to drop into a trash can.

Zonker Strip

A "Zonker strip" is a ribbon of tanned rabbit hide with fur (sometimes called a "rabbit strip"). The strip is cut in line with the slope of the fur. It is used on a fly called a Zonker, hence the name. Zonker strips are usually used as tails or to add fullness along the back of a fly. A "crosscut rabbit" strip is simply a hide-ribbon cut *across* the slope of the fur. Crosscut rabbit strips are wound up the shank to create full, shaggy bodies of fur that sweeps back.

1. Stretch the hide tight; then cut the Zonker or crosscut strips from its tanned side. Use a sharp blade (like this single-edge razor blade) and cut as shallow as possible. Never lay the hide on a flat surface to cut it—you'll end up cutting the tips off the fur.

CUTTING ZONKER STRIPS

Stretch the skin tight and then cut on the tanned side with a razor blade. One option is to lock one end of the skin in your tying vise.

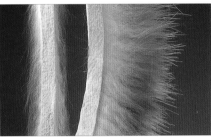

2. On the left is a Zonker strip, cut in line with the slope of the fur. On the right is a crosscut rabbit strip, with the fur sloping off the side of the strip.

V. FLOATING FLIES

All the flies included in this section float, but they do more than that. The Skip's Sputterface chugs and gurgles, the Deer Hair Mouse swims, the Messinger Bucktail Frog skips on the water and flips its hair-tip fins. Expect floating bass flies to vary in design and in how they perform and how they are fished.

Regardless of what floating bass flies do, it is important that they do it in a natural upright position. A good design helps achieve that. But there's a long-running debate about the way a hair bass-fly should be trimmed in order to keep the fly upright. Some tiers believe that trimming the hair along the underside of the fly only partway up to the hook's shank helps turn the fly over properly during the cast, and that wide-gape bass-fly hooks still leave plenty of room for the hook's point to do its work. Others, I among them, prefer to cut close, feeling that the fly will land upright just as consistently trimmed this way as any other and that the extra clearance around the point can only improve the odds of solid hook-ups. Cut close or not—with plenty of advocates for each approach you can't make a bad choice.

But you don't always get a choice. The Messinger Bucktail Frog must have a *round* body—literally a sphere from every angle of view, in order simply to *be* a Messinger Bucktail Frog. And this round body helps the fly bounce and skim across the water as it should. You could trim the Deer Hair Mouse close beneath, but you'd reduce the size of the white belly, which I don't see as a big deal, though some probably do. You can trim the underside of the Skip's Sputterface and most hair bass bugs close or out from the hook's shank as you prefer.

TYING DIFFICULTY
(1 is easy; 5 is difficult)

Skip's Sputterface	4
Deer Hair Mouse	5
Messinger Bucktail Frog	5

THE SKIP'S SPUTTERFACE

It's sealed, rubbery, concave mask makes the Skip's Sputterface unique among flared-hair bass bugs, and makes it especially effective for largemouth bass. This face scoops up water, resulting in a bug that makes lots of efficient fuss from only gentle tugs at the tippet, while not moving much from where it landed. Largemouth-bass often lie in tight cover—a tub-size opening among lily pads, a narrow slot between two fallen logs—consequently, a bug that announces it presence and then sticks around for the bass to show up is a winner.

A bug that makes a disturbance while holding its place has advantages with smallmouth too, but for different reasons. In smallmouth rivers the problem isn't normally tight cover; it's current sweeping the bug away before the bass get a look at it. The Skips Sputterface minimizes this problem.

I fish the Skip's Sputterface for largemouth bass just as I would most floating bass flies—a splat for a landing, a bit of commotion, a long pause, a twitch, a pause, a few feet of labored swimming, and then another cast to promising cover. However, if all goes well, I won't get through the whole sequence—a bass will intervene.

I fish the Skip's Sputterface for smallmouth bass also in the standard fashion, but standard *smallmouth* fashion, of course: gurgles of the fly separated by three- or four-second pauses, unless the bass are in an odd mood and want longer or shorter pauses.

Learn to tie the Skip's Sputterface and you learn to tie a standard hair bass bug—the only difference is the coating of silicone and cutting into the bug's face to create the depression. Hair bugs do vary in design. There are different kinds of tails and a few optional features. But although every slight variation in a trout fly seems to bring with it a new name—the Light Cahill, Dark Cahill, Hendrickson, and Red Fox dry flies, for example, all carry the same wings and hackles and tails and the same configuration and differ only in the colors of some of their parts—a bass bug is pretty much a bass bug. Tie one with a hackle tail and it's a bass bug. Tie one with a hackle tail and rubber-strand legs and plastic eyes and it's still just a bass bug, or at most "a bass bug with legs and eyes." A few patterns with unusual features, or just generous exposure, have maintained original names, but for every one of them there are perhaps a hundred other floating hair bass flies in all sorts of colors and variations that fall into the broad net of the term "bass bug."

So, here's your chance to put all that preparatory instruction on flaring and trimming hair to use. Have fun!

SKIP'S SPUTTERFACE

Hook: Heavy wire, short shank (bass-bug hook), a total hook-length of about 1 to 1 3/4 inches.

Thread: For the tail, 3/0 in the tail's color; for the body, any hair-flaring thread in white, gray, or the body's color.

Tail: Krystal Flash between four webby grizzly saddle hackles. The color of the tail should match or complement the color of the body. I have used gold Krystal Flash most often, but pearl or a color similar to the hackles' color makes sense.

Skirt: The tips of the body hair.

Body: Deer hair, of any standard bass-bug color—green, black, gray, purple, yellow, or tan—or whatever color you like.

Legs: Two to four rubber-strands. Half the strands match the color of the body or face and the other half match the color of the trim ring.

Trim Ring: Black deer hair, or some color different from the color of the body (a trim ring is optional).

Face: White deer hair saturated with silicone glue. (For a more subtle look, the face can be the same color as the body.)

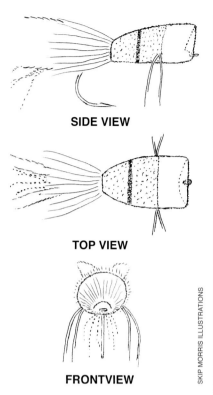

SIDE VIEW

TOP VIEW

FRONTVIEW

3. Whip finish the 3/0 thread in front of the mono, cut it, and then start some hair-flaring thread over the whip finish. Stack a modest-size bunch of deer or elk hair; then secure it along one side of the hook with a couple of only modestly tight thread-turns. The hair's tips should extend back from the thread-turns about one full hook-length or a bit less. Stack and bind another hair-bunch on the other side of the shank, hold *all* the hair firmly, and pull the thread tight.

6. Flare and compress white hair up to just short of the eye (or right up to it, if you skipped the snag guard) in one, or at most, two, bunches. Do not yet pull the thread forward through this last bunch of flared white hair.

1. Start the 3/0 thread. Bind some mono-filament along the bend if you want a snag guard. The forward end of the mono should lie just ahead of the bend; on most hooks, this would be directly over the point. Double three to five strands of Krystal Flash over the thread, and then bind them atop the snag-guard mono (or atop the shank, if you skipped a snag guard); all the ends of the Krystal Flash should now project back, off the bend.

4. Stroke back the butts of the hair, pull the thread forward, and add a few tight thread turns in front of the hair. Flare another hair-bunch and compress it back (see section III, "Flaring and Shaping Hair")—no need to stack this bunch. This next step is optional: Flare a small bunch of black hair (or any color that contrasts with the color of the body), and compress it back.

7. Part the hairs atop this last bunch forward and back from the thread-turns (you won't see these turns—they're buried— and the hair needn't be parted perfectly). Bind a small bunch of white hair atop the parted hair. Hold *all* the hair securely in place as you do this, to keep the new hair on top. This bunch adds density, which will be useful later. Now pull the hair back, pull the thread forward, make a few half hitches, and compress the hair back.

2. Bind a matched pair of hackles on each side of the Krystal Flash (or atop it; see "Hackle Tails" in section IV, "More Techniques"). The hackle-pair sets should curve away from one another, should have evened tips, and should equal about 1 1/2 to 2 full hook-lengths.

5. Flare and compress another bunch (or two), and then add two to four rubber-strands for legs (see "Rubber-Strand Legs" in section IV, "More Techniques").

8. Cut the thread closely. Trim the body to a taper, rounded in cross-section, as shown in the illustration (see "Flaring and Shaping Hair" in section III, "More Techniques").

9. With a razor blade, cut a half-circle into the bug's face just over and behind the hook's eye. You can pivot the flat of the blade on the hook's eye if you wish. The idea is to recess the bug's face, make it concave. From this angle you can see the recessed face and rounded body.

RECESSING THE FACE

14. Scrape off the excess glue from the sides of the bug. As you do, stroke the hairs forward, to restore the face to its original concave shape. Trim the rubber-strand legs long, 1 1/2 to 2 full hook-lengths. Trim the Krystal Flash a bit beyond the hackles' tips.

11. Work outdoors in a cross-breeze or just use some kind of effective ventilation for this next step. If you never know the smell of the silicone glue you'll use next, *that's* ideal.

With a toothpick, spread a thick layer of the glue all over the cupped face of the bug.

12. Work a layer of glue all around the sides of the bug's face, a layer about 1/4-inch wide. Push the point of the toothpick into the hairs to work the glue in all through the front of the face; stroke the point through the hairs—whatever saturates the hair with glue.

15. When the glue is set, trim the flange of glue that formed around the rim of the bug's face.

A Skip's Sputterface with a flat face (not recessed) and no silicone glue is really just a basic bass bug, the kind that has been the standard floating bass fly for decades.

10. Trim the edges of the bug's face to a neat, vertical line. Complete the snag guard, if you included one. Add head cement to the thread-turns at the hook's eye.

13. Scrape off the excess glue from the bug's face with long, flat strokes of the toothpick. Keep wiping the toothpick with a rag as you clean up the bug's face.

Here's an early version of the Skip's Sputterface that took me two bright, angry, nearly 20-pound silver salmon in an Alaska river. The heavy bass hook finally straightened, but despite the grinding of the fish's substantial teeth, the bug's silicone face came through undamaged. That's when I decided the silicone face was a good idea, and a durable feature.

THE DEER HAIR MOUSE

Chris Helm is a congenial fellow and a fine fly tier who's mad for deer hair. He processes and sells it, has developed a tool for compressing it on a hook, has made several videos about tying with it, and ties with it whenever conscious. I suspect Chris dreams of spending his next life as a deer, covered from hoof tops to ear tips, from muzzle to tip of stub-tail with drab, spiky hair. Life will be rich.

Among the flies Chris loves to tie is his Deer Hair Mouse. Chris developed his mouse from one he was taught by Billy Munn, whose name raises eyebrows among fly tiers. I continued the theme by altering Chris's tying-approach for the fly to suit my own. The result is a fly pattern whose tying has passed through a few experienced hands.

The obvious question in all this is, Do bass actually eat mice often enough to know what one is? Regarding largemouth bass, Chris told me that he's not sure whether "bass recognize mice as mice." I tend to agree; I've seen no evidence that mice commonly wind up swimming in largemouth-bass lakes. But this ultimately becomes a moot point, because Chris catches largemouths on his mouse all through the season, and I, too, have caught plenty of largemouths on it. Perhaps largemouths see more mice on their water than Chris or I do. In any case, the fly takes largemouth bass.

Smallmouth bass may be another matter. They often live in streams, streams that may flow through fields and forests where mice live. It's easy to imagine a mouse falling from a high bank into water that currents have scoured deep—specifically, holding water for hungry smallmouth. In *Fly Fishing for Smallmouth Bass*, author Harry Murray says he doubts that any mouse "that finds himself swimming past a smallmouth's feeding station ever makes it all the way across," provided, of course, that smallmouth is large enough to swallow mice. He summarizes: "A deer-hair pattern, fished in close to the banks with a slow, steady retrieve, will take many fine bass."

Chris says his Deer Hair Mouse "is also excellent for pike, for night fishing for big browns, and for rainbows in Alaska." Bottom line: a mouse-fly is worth having, and Chris's is a fine one.

If you find joy in raising the lid of a fly box to find lifelike flies nestled beneath it (which many of us do; fly fishing is not our duty but our pleasure, after all), then tie the pattern as shown. But if you just want an effective bare-bones imitation of a mouse and no more, skip the ears, whiskers, and eyes—bass are far less likely than anglers to fret over such details.

In fishing the Deer Hair Mouse you'd do well to remember that mice do not pop, chug, or dive. I can't prove this because I haven't actually seen a mouse swimming, but I can't even picture a popping, chugging mouse gliding swiftly underwater now and then like a dolphin. I asked my veterinarian wife and a veterinarian friend of ours about this. I said, "Have you seen mice swim?"

They looked puzzled for a moment, then said, "No."

I said, "Well, you trained around laboratory mice a lot in school, right?"

"No," said the veterinarians.

This was going nowhere and I was beginning to feel a little foolish. I tried a different angle. I asked, "Have you treated many mice?"

They said, in effect, "We've treated mice, but never for injuries caused by water sports." Now I had the sense that they weren't really *trying* to be helpful. They added something like, "And we've never used water therapy in mouse recovery."

I gave my next question some thought. It had to be good if I wanted to ever get out of this. I asked: "Okay…how do you *think* a mouse would swim?"

They both agreed: dog paddle. I thought, Thank God…finally!

As a kid I dog paddled before I realized there was any other way to swim, so I know it well. Therefore, my only slightly educated guess is that swimming mice plod along anxiously but quietly by dog paddling. Consequently, your Deer Hair Mouse should plod along quietly too. Of course if there is a steep bank along the water you're fishing, remember that a mouse falling from such a height is likely to hit the water with a plop, and that your Deer Hair Mouse can be made to do the same.

DEER HAIR MOUSE

Hook: Bass-bug style hook with a slightly longer shank than usual. Regarding hook-size, I simply tie it as small as I think a mouse might be, up to as large an imitation as the fish demand, or as I am comfortable casting.

Thread: Any hair-flaring thread, white or gray.

Tail: Gray or black Ultra Suede (you can find this in a fabric store). (For both the tail and ears, chamois or Bugskin do the job, but Chris is sold on Ultra Suede for his mouse.)

Body: White deer under, natural gray on top (Chris says that the body can be all gray, for simplicity).

Ears: Gray or black Ultra Suede (or chamois or Bugskin).

Eyes: Black wool yarn.

Whiskers: Moose-body hair.

Snag Guard: As with most bass flies, a snag guard is optional on the Deer Hair Mouse, but Chris avoids it on his mouse whenever possible.

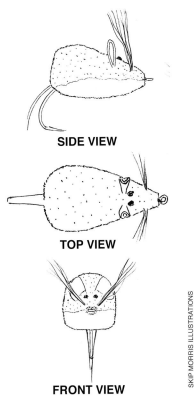

SIDE VIEW

TOP VIEW

FRONT VIEW

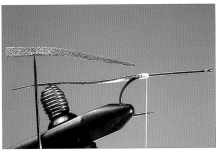

1. Start the hair-flaring thread tightly at the bend, and then bind on the tail there, atop the hook. Bind the tail over only a short section of the shank, leaving most of the shank clear for flaring hair. (Chris roughs up the hook at the bend with a round file to give the thread a texture to grip.) The tail should be at least 1 1/2 times as long as the entire hook and 1/8-inch wide at its base. The photo shows a tail bound on and another tail along its flat so you can see its shape.

2. With the thread hanging at the front of the tail-wraps, bind on a modest-size bunch of white deer. Rotate the deer to the underside of the hook and then pull the thread tight (see "Stacking Hair Colors" in section III, "Flaring and Shaping Hair").

3. Atop the white hair, bind a modest-size bunch of natural-gray hair. Part the ends of the top hair forward and back from the thread-turns that secure it (you won't actually see the thread—it's buried—and this needn't be perfect). In that part, bind a second bunch of gray hair atop the first with two turns of thread around all the hair and the shank—hold everything secure as you pull the thread tight, so the new bunch stays on top and all the other hair stays in place.

4. Flare and compress bunches of gray hair over bunches of white hair to slightly past halfway up the shank. Shape the body now. You can half hitch the thread and leave it uncut as you work or you can whip finish the thread, cut it, and then restart it later (this latter approach is the easier). Trim the body to a taper as shown. Leave plenty of hair underneath. Imaginary straight lines along the back and sides should just miss touching the hook's eye as they angle out. The rump and belly aren't critical, but the back and sides should be trimmed to final dimensions now.

PRESHAPE THE BODY

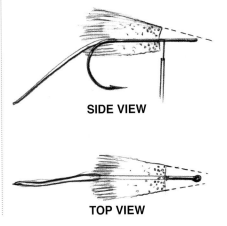

SIDE VIEW

TOP VIEW

5. Cut the ears from Ultra Suede as shown in the illustrations. Bind the ears atop the shank with crisscrossed turns of thread. Fold the ears so that their creases are inwards. Raise the ears as shown in the illustrations, and then compress the ears back into the body.

CUTTING OUT THE EARS

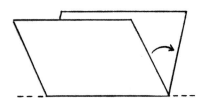

1. Fold a square of Ultra Suede in half and press that fold to a crease.

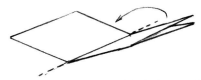

2. Fold and crease the doubled Ultra Suede again, this time across the first crease. The result should now be a square, about 1/4 the size of the original square.

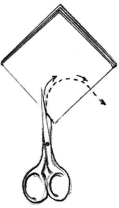

3. Cut a half-circle starting near the edge of the last crease and ending at the two creases, as shown in the illustration.

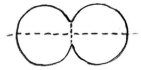

4. If all went well, unfolding the half-round shape should result in a pair of connected circles, as shown in the illustration.

MOUNTING AND SETTING THE EARS

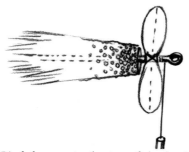

1. Bind the ears to the top of the hook's shank with two crisscrossed thread-turns.

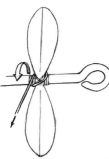

2. Wind the thread around the front of the far ear, and then back behind the ear. Pull the thread tight as you raise that ear to upright. The thread-direction is now reversed. Keep firm tension on the thread.

3. Set the near ear upright just as you set the far ear. Make a few tight thread-turns around the shank to lock everything in place. The thread should now be winding in its normal direction.

6. Flare and compress another bunch of gray hair over white. Make these bunches small, about one third the normal size. Whip finish the thread.

Carefully trim this new hair to its final shape. (Don't cut the thread for this, or for the next two times you flare and trim hair.)

7. Bind a length of yarn atop the shank with crisscrossed turns of thread. Add a couple of tight thread-turns around the shank. Take one turn of thread around *the ends of the yarn only*, to set them up in a shallow "V." Pull that turn tight; then add a couple of tight turns around the shank in front of the yarn. The ends of the yarn should now be up and close together. Compress the yarn back into the hair.

8. Flare and compress another bunch of gray hair over white; the bunches should be of standard size.

Trim this hair to its final shape.

9. Cut, comb, and stack a small bunch of moose-body hair, say 20 to 25 hairs. It's good to have a few extras as these moose-hairs are often accidentally cut while trimming the deer hair. Trim the hairs' butts straight across; the hairs should now about equal the length of the shank. Bind on the hair bunch by its butts atop the shank. Make the thread-turns close to the cut edge of the butts with the hair's tips projecting off the hook's eye. Divide the hairs into two groups of whiskers either by simply tugging the hairs into groups or with crisscrossed thread-turns.

10. Compress the whiskers back into the last flared hair; then flare and compress natural-gray hair over white hair once or twice more to reach the hook's eye. As usual, leave a bit of space behind the eye if you included a snag guard. Make a few half hitches in the thread and then trim it.

11. Trim the last bunches of compressed hair to shape—*but watch that you don't cut off the whiskers.* You can pull the whiskers up or down out of your way as you trim.

12. Trim the rear of the body to a plump, humped mouse-shape. Trim each of the ends of the yarn short, barely beyond the hair, as two black eyes. Complete the snag guard, if there is one. Add head cement to the finishing knot. If the ears are oversize or uneven, trim them.

13. Here's a no-frill's version of Chris's Deer Hair Mouse. Much easier to tie. Not impressive to anglers, but bass seem quite taken with it.

THE MESSINGER BUCKTAIL FROG

Joe Messinger Senior left the army and returned to his home in West Virginia at the end of World War I with the curious desire to create a frog-imitating fly for largemouth bass. War does strange things to men. Because fly-tying instruction of any kind was rare back then, this was a formidable task. But Joe had seen other flared-hair bass bugs and decided that with enough raw determination he could figure out how to make one. He did, and the hair-flaring technique he developed in the process—along with practically everything else about his Messinger Bucktail Frog—was and still is unique.

When Joe died, the loss of his father compelled Joe Messinger Jr. to master his father's frog, and he set himself to it for several months, relying on his father's past instruction and his own unique strain of the family genetics for raw determination.

Determination is handy in learning to tie the Messinger Bucktail Frog. It's the legs that really take practice. Besides helping the fly land upright on the water, the Messinger Bucktail Frog's springy legs give a delayed nervous flip after the fly is tugged. But the real marvel here for tiers is how Joe binds in and flares the hair on this fly with *knots* rather than with turns of thread in conventional fashion—no winding of thread at all during the flaring of the hair. This, his father's approach, creates a tightly packed body and is a good solution for the problem of keeping the top-hair and belly-hair separated.

Even the plastic eyes on the Messenger Bucktail Frog are unique. Joe forms them by melting plastic in acetone, and then shaping each eye between his fingers.

Tying the Messinger Bucktail Frog as Joe Junior, or Senior, would tie it is complex and so unorthodox that it could make a small volume by itself. I finally decided that it didn't make sense to squeeze another book into this book. So I went with conventional hair-color stacking for the body. But I can assure you that the modified frog to come will look and perform as does the original. If you want to learn to tie the Messinger Bucktail Frog with the same intriguing techniques used by the Joes, Joe Junior produced a very thorough video, though it's out of print now and might take some hunting to find.

We'll make the unique spring-loaded legs differently than the Joes would, but these legs will look and function just as the originals do. And we'll use premade eyes instead of the Joes' handmade ones.

Finding the right hair for the legs can be a challenge. It mustn't be too long. But the real test comes when you push the hair toward the hide—the hair should kink, not bend. This hair is found at the base of a buck's tail; it is somewhere between body hair and tail hair, and most tails lack it altogether. I have found that hard, stiff elk hair makes a passable substitute. Hard buck tail is barely adequate, and you will probably have to cover its butts with thread, as it won't flare. No substitute really gives the legs the recoil of just the right buck tail. But bass seem willing to overlook stiff or limp legs on the fly. Still, there's something about that flip of the fins on a proper Messinger Bucktail Frog.

Joe Senior tied his frog in two styles he called the meadow frog and the bleeding frog. The meadow-frog style has a golden-brown back and leg-tops, yellow for the underside of the legs and the first bunch of belly hair, white for the remainder of the belly. The bleeding-frog style has brown on top, red under the legs and for the rear of the belly, white for the rest of the belly. Joe Junior added a green frog with green top, yellow under the legs and rear of the belly, and white for the rest of the belly. I've also seen Joe Junior tie a frog with green on top and all-white underneath, and that's the one I'll tie here.

The Messinger Bucktail Frog is fished, as you'd expect, in a manner that mimics the action of a real frog. So there is no attempt to create a big disturbance; the fly's movement across the surface of the water should be a series of tiny quick skids with an occasional pause. With a well-executed tug, this frog-fly almost hops on the water.

MESSINGER BUCKTAIL FROG

Hook: Heavy wire, short shank (bass-bug hook), a total hook length of about 1 1/8 to 1 1/2 inches.

Thread: For the legs and for flaring the body-hair, any hair-flaring thread; for tension-setting the legs, black (or white or green) cotton-covered polyester carpet thread (this comes from a fabric or sewing store).

Legs: Buck tail of a color matching the top of the body for the tops of the legs, yellow or white or red for the undersides of the legs. The knees are created over a plated brass pin (which you can buy at a fabric or sewing store); a conventional straight pin is an adequate substitute.

Body: Dark deer hair (or elk) on top and light underneath. See the introduction above for color combinations.

Eyes: Large premade solid-plastic eyes, gold or yellow with black pupils (or hollow plastic eyes).

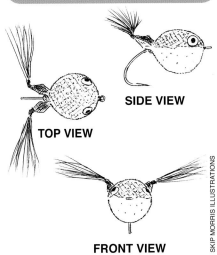

SIDE VIEW

TOP VIEW

FRONT VIEW

SKIP MORRIS ILLUSTRATIONS

1. For the legs, you want buck tail that is soft enough and short enough so its butts will flare almost as deer hair flares; this hair usually comes from the base of the tail. A good test is to cut off hairs close to the hide, and then push the ends together—the right hair will kink, as in the photograph, rather than bend. But you needn't cut off the hair to test it; you can do that by just pushing the hair into the hide—which of course means you won't have to buy every buck tail you test.

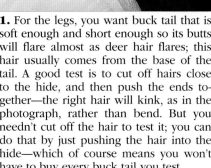

2. Bind on the monofilament snag guard, if you want one (see section II, "Snag Guards"). If you do bind on a snag guard, it should end at the very start of the bend, not on the shank. Start some hair-flaring thread (either green or white for this frog) at the bend. Snip off, comb, and stack a small bunch of white buck tail. Bind it on near its butts, its tips pointing *forward*, over and beyond the hook's eye. The hair should extend two shank-lengths from its tie-in point. Secure the hair with two turns of thread. Pull the turns half-tight, and then use the thread to push the hair around and finally under the hook.

3. Push your finger or thumb straight down onto hair and shank, and then pull the thread really tight. This locks the hair in place and keeps it from creeping up over the shank or mixing with the top hair.

4. Unwind the thread one half turn. Loop a few inches of the carpet thread around the flaring-thread, slide the loop of carpet thread down to the hook, and then rewind the half-turn of flaring-thread. Add another tight turn of flaring-thread from the other angle—so that the flaring-thread crisscrosses the carpet thread, and the ends of the carpet thread stick straight out to the sides.

CREATING THE LEGS

1. Bind the underside hair atop the hook with two turns of thread. Rotate the hair under the hook; then tighten the thread.

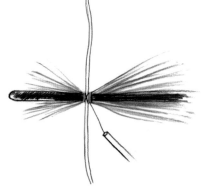

2. Unwind the working thread one half turn. Secure a few inches of carpet thread atop the shank with two crisscrossed turns of the working thread. The carpet thread should now be bound over the thread-turns holding the hair.

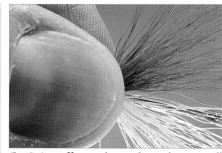

5. Snip off, comb, and stack a small bunch of green buck tail (about equal to the white). Bind it in over the white with two only modestly tight thread-turns. The carpet thread should be in front of the thread-turns securing the green buck tail. Pinch all the buck tail at its sides, and then pull the thread tight.

Getting the right amount of buck tail for the legs takes some practice. Note that this frog will have thin legs; the completed frog at the top of this section has thick legs. Either is fine, or anywhere in between.

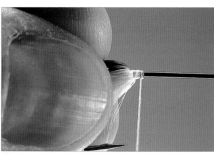

6. As you maintain thread-tension, draw back all the hair-tips and the carpet thread, pull the thread tightly forward, and then add four tight thread-turns against the front of the hair. Whip finish the flaring-thread, or add two half hitches, and then cut it.

7. Remove the hook from your vise. Stroke all the hair-tips and the loose ends of the carpet thread forward. Trim the butts of the buck tail to a tiny hump that tapers up from the shank forward (note that the hook is reversed in the vise).

8. Draw and stroke the hair tips and carpet thread back along the hook's bend. Start some thread (3/0 or size-A) over the buck tail and carpet thread (which is easier than it sounds) and make a snug (not tight) thread-band slightly down the bend. Whip finish and trim the thread. This is temporary and serves only to keep the shank clear for flaring hair. Restart the hair-flaring thread over the place you whip finished and cut it earlier, just ahead of the buck tail.

9. Flare and compress deer or elk hair, green over white, to the hook's eye. (See section III, "Flaring and Shaping Hair.") If you included a snag guard, leave a little space behind the eye in which to complete it.

10. Trim the hair to a more-or-less round shape. Leave slightly more hair beneath the hook than on top, but leave adequate space between the body and the hook's point, as in the photos. (The key to making a round body that doesn't block the point is to keep that body fairly short—beginning over the hook's point and ending just back from the hook's eye.)

11. Carefully cut one of the strands of the thread-band holding back the buck tail, and then remove that thread entirely, freeing the buck tail and carpet thread.

12. Divide the buck tail to the sides, into two distinct bunches. Pull the loose ends of the carpet thread back and work one end inside each bunch (keep the thread ends on their original sides).

13. Work a plated-brass pin into one bunch of buck tail. Pinch the hair, carpet thread, and pin together, and then, somehow, hold the end of some green or dark size-A rod-winding thread in the same hand (it really can be done). The rod-thread should be in a bobbin. Wind the rod-thread around all this in tight turns. The result should be a tight band of thread, about 1/4-inch wide and about one third of the way up the buck tail from the hook. Whip finish the thread and trim both its ends. Build a thread-band around the other hair bunch, pin, and carpet thread.

14. Gently—so as not to cut or break the thread—bend the pin in each buck-tail leg so that the flared tips angle forward and slightly up. I hold one end of the thread-band in a pair of round-nose pliers and push the other end against my thumb (though I couldn't get my thumb into the photograph).

15. Hold the thread-band of one leg as you pull on the loose end of the carpet thread. Do the same to the other leg. This loads each leg under tension, giving it its spring and filling it out. It doesn't take much thread-pulling to do the job; refer to the photographs.

16. Coat the thread-bands with cement—Joe uses "Bug Glaze," I use epoxy glue. I blast the epoxy with a hand-held hair dryer on full heat (outdoors in a cross-breeze to keep from breathing the vapors). This causes the epoxy to thin and really saturate the size-A thread, carpet thread, and hair.

17. When the coating over the leg-band thread is fully hardened, bend back the hair at the joints to expose the ends of the pins. Cut the pins closely, at both ends of each joint. Trim the carpet thread close to each leg-joint. If you are using a snag guard, complete it at the eye with 3/0 thread. Snag guard or no, add head cement just behind the eye.

18. To complete the Messinger Bucktail Frog, snip out a socket on each side of the top-front of the body and glue an eye into each. (Joe prefers the solid-plastic eyes shown on the completed fly at the beginning of this section, but the hollow plastic eyes shown here are an option. See "Eyes, Hollow or Solid-Plastic, Glueing on" in section IV, "More Techniques").

VI. SINKING FLIES

Weather can bless or curse your fishing. The wrong weather can turn wading a river or going out in a boat into peril. The right weather, of course, can provide good fishing all day, ideally with you as comfortable and enthusiastic as the fish.

Beyond its dangerous extremes, weather is largely about the barometer when it comes to bass fishing. Mild weather raises the barometer tending to make largemouth and smallmouth bass, and pan-fishes too, happy and ready for a floating or diving fly. Stormy weather sends the barometer down, and bass, and pan fish, typically go down with it. This is one good time to turn to sinking flies.

A low or falling barometer isn't the only thing that will send bass to the depths—midday heat, glaring sunlight, and too-warm water can do the same. When bass are deep, only a sinking fly will take them. Sometimes it isn't so much that bass are deep as that they are dour—I've seen largemouth bass lying only three feet down yet unwilling to rise near the surface. But they'd take a Clouser Minnow or Shineabou Sunfish darting down in front of their eyes. If you're new to bass fly fishing, get used to the reality of bass shunning the water's surface. Happens pretty often.

Sinking flies offer a big bonus: big bass. Largemouth in particular, I've found, seldom feed on top once they reach about three pounds. So, although there are exceptions, expect sinking flies to account for those precious few bass each season that swell your pupils and strain your biceps.

Floating bass flies provide a show, everything—the dance of the fly, the bite or smack of the bass—all in full view. But sinking flies hold the fascination of reaching down into invisible depths and all the possibilities of the imagination.

TYING DIFFICULTY	
(1 is easy; 5 is difficult)	
Clouser Minnow	2
Skip's Hover Bug	3
Grim Reaper	4
Hare Waterpup	5
Shineabou Sunfish	5

THE CLOUSER MINNOW

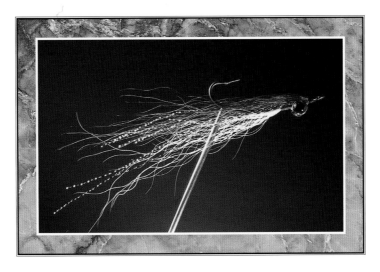

Some time around the mid-80s, Bob Clouser handed a forerunner of the Clouser Deep Minnow to his friend Lefty Kreh. Lefty, the renowned fly-fishing author, speaker, and pioneer, turned the little brush of hair and hook in the light, and began to see in it real potential. From there, Lefty and Bob together developed the version of the fly so popular today. Their Clouser Minnow (we usually leave off the "Deep" nowadays) was originally for smallmouth bass. But as Lefty traveled the world in search of all those fishes he might pursue with a fly, he carried along Clouser Minnows. Three years after he and Bob had finished their work on the fly, Lefty'd caught 58 species of freshwater and saltwater fishes on Clousers.

But despite those 58 species and all the others since, I imagine that even today more Clouser Minnows are fished for smallmouth than for all other fishes combined. Clousers and smallmouth just seem a natural pairing.

But Clousers are excellent for largemouth bass too. Lefty once told me that for largemouth he ties his Clousers fuller than usual, to suit these fish's preference for corpulent fare. So I tied some *thicker* (though still pretty thin) Clousers and took them to a nearby largemouth lake. I've been tying such Clousers and taking them largemouth fishing ever since—they work.

Still, it's mainly smallmouth I've taken on Clousers. And I've worked out a few ways of doing so. But one of the more intriguing methods I use is my wife's.

Carol's intuition with smallmouth seems a match for her intuition with cats and dogs—she's a veterinarian, so this is *some* intuition. Back in the early 90s I introduced her to smallmouth bass by showing her a few techniques I used with the Clouser Minnow, and then turning her loose on the river. By the time we'd found each other again, she'd figured out some things. She pointed her rod at a backwater and asked, "See the fish?" I peered into the still, clear water at a row of three curious ten-inch smallmouth staring back. They and we were keenly aware of each other, so it seemed an extremely unlikely situation in which to hook bass on Clousers or anything else.

She explained: "They're like cats are with birds—lots of instinct and not much willpower. You just can't give them time to think." She turned to the three fish and flicked the little Clouser out past them, let it

sink a couple of feet, and then teased it in. The Clouser swam up from behind a staring bass to within inches from its tail, then was nearly next to its eye when the fish turned savagely. "You see?" she said with a laugh, pulling on the bouncing rod, "instinct."

There are other ways to fish a Clouser. Because it rides with its bend up, it can usually drop right onto the bottom and then swim up without snagging. This opens up a lot of options. Sometimes smallmouth really go for a Clouser darting up from the bottom, or dropped onto the bottom and then swum up off it after a twitch or two. But the reliable standard approach is still just to get the fly down and then simply swim it steadily along, teasing the slender, flexible wing into quivers and waves.

I've tied Clousers on a variety of hooks—long shank, regular shank, even light-wire dry-fly hooks—and all have worked well. But for smallmouth, I find it hard to beat the standard-wire, slow-curve, 2X long hooks with straight eyes, such as the Tiemco 200 and Daiichi 1260. Logic says a down-eye hook would lower the center of gravity in the fly and better insure the fly of a proper inverted posture in the water, but the straight-eye slow-curve hooks ride right and bite and hold, so I don't question them.

Lefty prefers buck tail for the wings of large Clousers, and supple fox tail in the wings of small ones. (Some tiers like squirrel tail for small Clousers.) Incidentally, Lefty told me that he experimented with leaving some of the Krystal Flash or Flashabou slightly longer than the wing and now prefers it this way. Fact is, everyone seems to tie the Clouser Minnow with his or her own mix of materials, colors, and proportions. Everyone should—a little creativity can make the Clouser imitate all kinds of fresh and saltwater bait fishes.

Many smallmouth fly fishers like Clousers with chartreuse wings and white bellies. I've had my best success with natural Clousers like the baby-bass version below. Try both.

Size? Depends, of course, on the size of your smallmouth. For eight- to twelve-inch fish I use Clousers of size 10 and 8; for large smallmouth, size 6 and 4. (These sizes are based on 2X long hooks, so hooks would theoretically be one size smaller if 3X long and two sizes smaller if 4X long.) For largemouth bass, just tie your Clousers *big* with strong hooks.

CLOUSER DEEP MINNOW
(my baby-bass version)

Hook: Heavy wire, 2x to 4X long, sizes 10 to 2.
Thread: Brown 3/0.
Eyes: Lead or lead-substitute barbell eyes (preferably red with black pupils for a baby smallmouth, and medium-brown with black pupils for a baby largemouth).
Belly: White buck tail (other versions use other light colors and even synthetic strands).
Under Wing: Gold Krystal Flash or Flashabou (or some other bright synthetic strands).
Wing: Brown buck tail (other versions use other dark, light, or bright colors and even synthetic strands).

1. The Clouser uses lead or lead-substitute barbell eyes. Here are a few options, from left to right: (1) this style comes with its eyes mounted at the ends of a bright-metal form, (2) these barbell eyes, like the ones on the far right, came without actual eyes, but I peeled adhesive-backed eyes from the sheet of such eyes shown in the photo, pressed the eyes onto the ends of the barbell eyes, and coated everything (outdoors, with good ventilation) with epoxy glue, (3) this barbell form comes with eyes already painted on, (4) another eyeless barbell form, its ends roughened with sandpaper to best hold the tier's paints (any paint, even kids' non-toxic paints, will do the job after a coating of epoxy glue...applied with good ventilation).

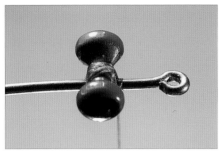

2. Bind on the eyes about 1/8" back from the hook's eye with lots of tight crisscrossing turns of thread (see "Eyes, Barbell, Binding on" in section IV, "More Techniques").

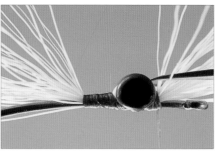

4. Draw the buck tail's butts up and back, and then advance the thread to just in front of the stem of the barbell eyes. Bind and trim the buck tail's butts in front of the eye-stem.

The buck tail should not be pulled tight over the eyes' stem—that will only make it fragile. Better if the hair is under only light tension.

6. Invert the hook in your vise. Loop three to eight strands of Krystal Flash (or Flashabou or both) over the thread and secure them just in front of the barbell eyes. Draw all the Krystal Flash back and bind it. All its ends should now sweep back, off the bend. Remember—now that the hook is inverted, everything is bound on *ahead* of the barbell eyes.

3. Bind a small amount of buck tail atop the shank, just behind the barbell eyes. Because the Clouser rides with its hook inverted, this hair forms the fly's belly. The tips of the hair should project back over and off the bend.

Don't stack the buck tail. The longest hairs should project about two full hooklengths from where they are bound on; this will also be the length of the wing. (Some tiers make some good arguments for keeping the belly-hair shorter than the wing-hair. An option.)

5. The finished belly hair bound on both sides of the stem of the barbell eyes. (Note the bare fibers humped over the stem.)

7. Bind the dark buck tail on atop the Krystal Flash. The buck tail should project back two hook-lengths from where it is bound, which is the same length as the buck-tail belly. Trim the butts of the buck tail to a taper, build a thread head, whip finish and trim the thread.

The wing on this fly should be sparse (although, as I mentioned, thicker for largemouth bass); a sparse wing lets the fly sink quickly and is more flexible and active than a dense wing. Lefty says that "on a Clouser Deep Minnow dressed on a size two hook, the total wing, when compressed, should have a diameter no larger than a barn burner wooden match."

A hefty smallmouth still pinned to a Clouser Minnow.

8. Trim the Krystal Flash to various lengths (Lefty leaves a few strands slightly longer than the buck tail). Add head cement to the thread head.

THE SKIP'S HOVER BUG

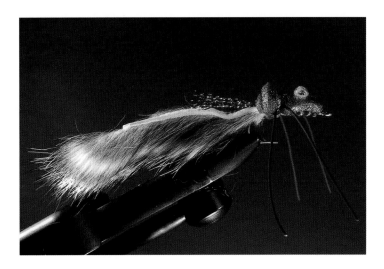

The Skip's Hover Bug does, in fact, hover (and swim and dart) just above lake-bed snags, which happens to be an excellent place to find smallmouth and largemouth bass—when they're out in the depths, these fishes usually hold close to the lake's bed. The idea is, a fast-sinking fly line finds the bottom while this buoyant fly rises just above it to swim and dart and wave its billowy tail. Yes, the line will sink down among tall, sparse water plants and snag the fly in them, and there are other situations that will mess the thing up. But on the whole, this concept that to experienced fly fishers would seem far too neat and logical to actually work, does work—over a fairly clear lake bed I've fished this fly for an hour, hooking fish steadily without once hooking the bottom.

After all, you can't catch bass on a fouled fly—and who wants to spend half their fishing time coaxing free a snagged fly and clearing its hook?

I designed the Skip's Hover Bug for largemouth bass in lakes, and it's proven itself there. Recently I've been experimenting with the fly in smallmouth-bass lakes. The results are promising.

To the best of my knowledge, the monofilament stiffener for the tail is unique. It grew from some experiments with trailer hooks for short takes. I gave up on the trailer, but the monofilament clearly reduced the typical fouling of the rabbit-strip tail with the point and bend of the hook.

The color-combinations you see here are but two of many. Actually, I have used all-black (all-black except for the tuft of gold Krystal Flash) most often. But I've had success with yellow and gray and other colors. Bottom line: keep an open mind about colors for Hover Bugs. I normally use gold Krystal flash over the rabbit-strip, but that can be altered, and the eyes needn't be yellow, although I do prefer hollow eyes over solid-plastic ones— hollow eyes are buoyant. But this fly is naturally buoyant enough to fish perfectly well with no eyes at all.

Because the Skip's Hover Bug floats, I have occasionally fished it on the surface, usually because some worthwhile largemouth splashed in the shallows and I just couldn't pass it up, but wasn't willing to switch lines and abandon good deep-water fishing. Because of these occasional events, I've learned that the Hover Bug actually works as a floating fly, but I still think it's best fished deep.

Nearly always I fish it well down, actively, with brief pauses. I keep it active because detecting a bass's take can be difficult on a slow retrieve of the fly—a bass can mouth a fly without moving it. But if a bass mouths a moving fly, the angler will feel the resistance.

To best fish the Skip's Hover Bug, play with it, and observe. Let the line take it down a few inches. Its supple tail undulates softly, long after the rest of the fly is still. Tug the line—the rubber strands sweep back, then swing slowly out again. Make the fly move in a series of darts; the legs and tail respond differently than before, yet still are lively. Now you can see, in your mind, the movements of the fly as you work it over the bottom. That's always an advantage.

1. Cut a strip of rabbit hide about 1/8" wide (wider if you like). The strip's fur should be intact, and the fur should slope along the strip's length. Trim the end of the strip, the end towards which the fur slopes, to a point. The easy way is to buy precut rabbit-hide strips; they are usually called "Zonker strips" or something similar (see "Zonker Strips" in section IV, "More Techniques").

2. Trim the strip to a total length of slightly more than two full hook-lengths. Trim the fur away from the hide to about 1/4 inch back from the cut end, the end *from* which the fur slopes, the opposite end from the now-pointed one.

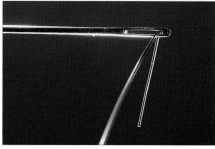

5. Bend one end of the mono and slip it through the eye of a big needle.

8. Give the hide-strip a modest tug near its point. This is to adjust the mono loop to length; usually the loop will slip out slightly. Bind the ends of the mono now with tight thread-turns. Trim the butt-ends of the mono.

3. Start the thread at the hook's bend. Make a short layer of tight thread-turns over the rear of the shank. Bind the fur strip atop the hook by the end of its hide, at the bend. The fur should slope away from the hook. The bare hide should face up, the fur down.

6. Push the needle downward through the bare side of the hide, about halfway between the pointed tip of the hide and the hook. Push the needle back up through the hide about 1/4 inch toward the hook. Pull the needle through the hide (I grasp the needle with flat-nose pliers), drawing the mono with it. For the first puncture, I grasp the hide just behind the point of the needle; for the second puncture, I grasp the hide just *ahead* of the needle's point with the hide pulled back behind the point. This strategy keeps my fingers away from the needle's sharp point and protects my blood supply.

9. Double three to five strands of Krystal Flash over the thread and then slide them down to the hook and bind them atop it. Draw the strands back and secure them to project over the rabbit strip. Trim the strands short, no longer than the end of the mono loop.

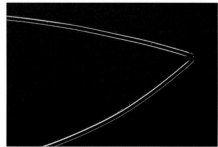

4. Kink about eight inches of monofilament leader at its middle. You want a permanent sharp bend in the mono—I often give it a light squeeze with flat-nose smooth-jaw pliers to really set it. The stiffness of the mono seems important—too stiff will stiffen the tail too much and impede hook penetration, too supple will allow the tail to catch on the hook's point. I've been using 8-pound Maxima on smaller hooks with good results, but please feel free to experiment.

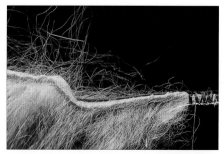

7. Bind the ends of the mono lightly at the hook's bend. The bend in the center of the mono should lie above or in the hole in the hide that is farthest from the hook.

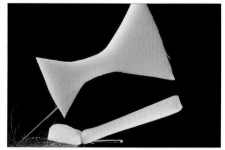

10. Cut the body from a thick sheet of soft, buoyant closed-cell foam. The piece of foam suspended over the hook is a sample—a small triangle at one end; a slim stretch that's slightly shorter than the shank; and a large triangle at the other end.

Bind the foam atop the hook's bend, near the small triangle. The small triangle should project back, over the bend, and the large triangle should project forward.

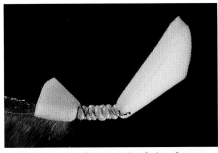

11. Draw the front end of the foam up and back from the shank. Wind the thread forward to right up against the hook's eye. Lower the foam and secure it just behind the eye with lots of firm, not tight, thread-turns (tight turns can cut the foam). Wind the thread back to the bend, securing the foam along the shank in the process.

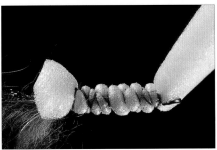

12. Trim the end of the small triangle to a short fan.

13. Draw the front end of the foam up and back, and then secure it at the hook's bend with several firm turns of thread.

14. Trim the fan of foam, the new one that was formed when you bound the large foam-triangle back, to a *short* fan.

15. Loop a few inches of rubber-strand over the thread, slide the strand up the thread to one side of the foam, and then secure the strand with a few tight thread-turns. Add a few inches of rubber-strand on the other side of the foam in this same manner. There should now be two lengths of rubber-strand projecting from each side of the foam. Draw the strands back, add a Skip's whip (see "Skip's Whip" in section IV, "More Techniques"), and trim the thread.

16. If the foam needs coloring, do so now with a marking pen, but leave an uncolored spot on each side of the foam for the eyes.

Bass flies from long ago. They were photographed at the Cushner Museum.

17. Glue an eye to each side of the body. (I use partly cured low-vapor epoxy glue with good ventilation, though I'm sure other glues would work.) Trim the rubber-strands to about two full hook-lengths.

THE GRIM REAPER

Pat Ehlers's Grim Reaper is a hit bass fly; I was told so by both Bob Story and Mike Mercer. Bob owns and manages Feather-Craft Fly-Fishing in St. Louis, Missouri; Mike (along with owner Mike Mikulak) manages The Fly Shop in Redding, California—these are two big, highly respected fly-fishing mail-order operations, and the guys who run them should know which flies are hot.

The fly is an eyeful: a broad leechy tail, a sparkling shaggy body, a collar of waving rubber tentacles, all pulled together on, of all things, a jig hook. A jig-hook fly isn't so freakish now as it was a decade ago—a few other current popular patterns, including John Barr's Meat Whistle and another Ehlers fly, the Foam Tail Superworm (both are in section XIII, "Additional Bass and Pan-Fish Flies"), are tied on jig hooks. But it's still rare enough to rate as a curiosity among most fly fishers.

That may be changing. For the past couple of decades a number of tiers have been working to design underwater flies that flip over—the Clouser Minnow is a perfect example— and they're discovering that the jig hook, with any weight added to it at all, makes the flip a cinch.

Pat developed his Reaper off of a bass lure—a true "lure," cast on monofilament line rather than fly line—commonly called a "jig-n-pig," a jig with a supple tail that used to be made of real pig skin. Now in place of the pig skin is a rubbery and wormlike long-bladed tail that waves and flips, called a reaper tail. For his Grim Reaper, Pat replaced this rubbery tail with a strip cut from supple leathery sheeting that also waves and flips and is, I'm guessing, more durable than the original reaper tail.

The Grim Reaper is a fly for both largemouth and smallmouth bass. You can toss it out to sink and then swim and bump its way through lily pad stalks in a largemouth lake, or throw it into the current of a smallmouth river to skim the tops of boulders—either way it's unlikely to snag anything with its hook point turned up.

That's the biggest advantage of flies that ride upside down—they tend to hook fish as well as (some would say better than) upright flies but with far less chance of snagging a rock or sunken tree limb or whatever else happens to be down there. And when it comes to largemouth bass in particular, tossing a fly into a mine field of potential snag-ups is often the most productive strategy. Another advantage of the inverted fly is that the bend and point of the hook may be obscured or hidden altogether by the wing or whatever other waving material is streaming back, making the fly all that much more convincing. But this second matter doesn't get much attention—it's that snag-resistance that turns the heads of so many fly fishers who've lost so many flies to weeds and boulders and sunken brush.

Pat considers his root beer version a sometimes crayfish imitation. The Fire/Tiger version seems clearly an attractor design—but chartreuse is a hot fly color these days for smallmouth and largemouth both.

This is a different fly at the tying vise than any other presented in this book. And not just because it's tied on a jig hook—it's got that peculiar rattle to work around and a peculiar rubber-strand collar created in a simple and sensible way that distributes the strands neatly. It's not a terribly difficult fly to tie, but it'll take some getting used to.

Bass flies with rattles, following a trend in bass lures, have been showing up for at least 15 years. Bass, and most fish, "hear," if you want to call it that, very well. They feel the vibrations we call sound with a row of sensory organs along each of their sides, their "lateral lines." Water is much denser than air and consequently carries sound much better than air does—that's why it's so easy to spook fish when you bang an oar on a submerged rock or wade clumsily into the water. The rattle gives the bass a sound from the fly that varies in a living way. Bass anglers who use conventional spinning and casting rods believe that rattles both catch bass's attention and sound like some of the things they eat. I'm not convinced either way yet, so I consider the rattle optional. But I normally tie my Grim Reapers with the rattle; I figure Pat knew what he was doing when he added it.

I also tie my Grim Reapers a little differently than Pat ties his. His way is rock-solid. Mine is just a few stylistic tweaks from his.

The world of bass flies is growing ever stranger, and Pat's jig-hook, tentacle-waving, rattle-clicking Grim Reaper makes that point. But bass fishing was never mainly about imitation. Sure, largemouth and smallmouth bass can lock their sights on a particular minnow or a dragonfly nymph or any number of other creatures to the exclusion of all else. I've seen it many times. Usually, though, bass are convinced not so much by imitation as by presentation, by how natural and alive the fly behaves. With its tentacles flipping and body shimmering and supple tail seeming to paddle the thing along, it's a fly that wants to look alive. You just have to get it in front of a bass and give it a little help.

You can learn more about Pat's Grim Reaper and his other bass-fly designs from his DVD, "Tying the Flies of Pat Ehlers, Bass Flies."

GRIM REAPER, FIRE TIGER

Hook: Heavy wire jig hook, size 3/0 (I sometimes tie it smaller, for smallish bass). Pat prefers a "60° jig hook," but I often use a standard jig hook with a 90° kink like the one in the photos.

Thread: Chartreuse 6/0 or 3/0.

Tail: Large Hairline Dubbin' Fish Reaper Tail, chartreuse (or cut the tail from chamois, thin leather, or Ultrasuede).

Eyes: Medium to large lead barbell eyes painted chartreuse with black pupils.

Rattle (optional): Glass rattle, 3 to 5 mm.

Body: Chartreuse UV Polar Chenille (or another sparkling hairy rope or picked-out dubbing).

Collar: Hot Tipped Crazy Legs in "Yellow/Chart./Fl. Orange Tipped" (or another chartreuse rubber-strand that you can color on the ends with a permanent orange marking pen).

GRIM REAPER, ROOT BEER

Tied below. The hook is the same size and design as for the Fire Tiger version, as is the rattle. Thread is red, barbell eyes are red, Reaper Tail is "Rusty Brown," UV Polar Chenille is "Rusty Copper," collar is Crazy Legs in "Brown/Orange Flake."

1. Start the thread halfway up the hook's shank, and then wind it tightly in close turns down the shank to the bend. Pinch the narrow tab-end of a reaper tail down around the top of the shank and bind it there, directly in front of the bend. Hold the tail down against the bend and wind the thread tightly down the bend just a little ways, only about 1/16 to 1/8 inch, to bind a little bit of the tail where it swells out from the tab—this makes the tail tougher and angles it down (eventually, up). Bind the tail's tab-end tightly up the shank.

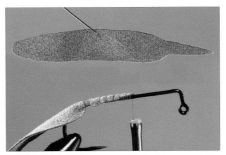

2. If you cut your own Grim Reaper tails, follow the shape of the Reaper Tail at the top of the photo. The tail should be about 1 1/3 times the full length of the hook (not including the tab by which the tail is bound) and about 2/3 the width of the hook's gape.

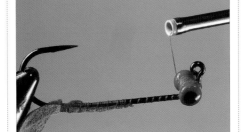

3. Spiral the thread tightly up to where the shank kinks below the hook's eye. Turn the hook upside down in your vise. Bind the barbell eyes there on *top* of the shank in the kink. Use lots of tight criss-crossed thread-turns.

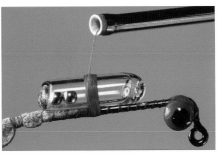

4. Spiral the thread back to the center of the shank. Turn the fly right-side-up in your vise. Hold the rattle atop the shank so its center lies directly over the hanging thread. Bind the rattle with a slim band of thread (about 20 tight turns). (Pat feels that binding the rattle from end to end kills its sound.)

5. Wind turns of thread under the ends of the rattle and around the band of thread, pulling each turn tightly up to the thread-band—these turns will lock the rattle on top of the shank. (If the thread won't slip up to the thread-band, pull up on the end of the rattle briefly to reduce the pressure and let the thread slip through.)

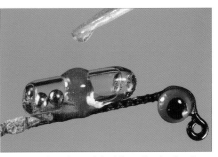

6. Coat the thread holding both the barbell eyes and the rattle with head cement or low-vapor epoxy—better yet, whip finish and cut the thread, build several flies to this point, then coat them all at once, and then resume tying the next day.

7. Spiral the thread back to the bend (or, if you cut the thread before adding the epoxy, restart the thread behind the rattle first). Hold the end of a length of Polar Chenille (at least two feet) and stroke the fibers back at least 1/4-inch down from the end, the end from which the shiny strands slope. Bind the Polar Chenille by at least its last 1/4-inch atop the bend of the hook. Bind the end tightly over its length, up the shank, with plenty of tight turns of thread.

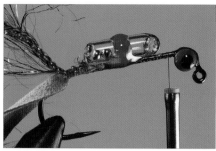

8. Spiral the thread to the rattle and then steeply forward under the shank to the front of the rattle, and then in closer spirals to the rear of the eyes.

9. Polar Chenille has a side that's mostly bare and another side with most of the fibers. Work the Polar Chenille around so that as you wind it, the bare side lies against the shank and the full side is turned out.

Stroke back the fibers of the Polar Chenille after each turn to keep them clear of being caught and bound under the next turn.

10. Wind the Polar Chenille firmly up the shank in close turns to the rear of the rattle.

Right behind the rattle, wind tight turns of the Polar Chenille atop one another (angle the turns back under the end of the rattle if needed) until the Polar Chenille climbs up onto the rattle. (With a 5mm rattle and a 3/0 hook, this could require a dozen or more turns.)

11. Wind the Polar Chenille up the rattle and then off its very end in front.

12. Build turns of the Polar Chenille tightly against the front of the rattle (again angling it back under the end of the rattle)—this will prevent the Polar Chenille from sliding forward off the rattle under the rigors of fishing.

13. Wind the Polar Chenille forward in close turns to the rear of the barbell eyes. Bind the end of the Polar Chenille tightly with plenty of thread-turns right behind the barbell eyes, and then trim off the end of the Polar Chenille.

14. If you're using Crazy Legs, cut one of the sections of the strands in half crossways—this should leave you with two sections of strands, each around three inches long, with each section attached at a tab-end.

15. Pinch the free, cut ends of one of the sections of strands into a flat row and hold them down against the top of the shank right behind the eyes. Try to roll the strands around the top half of the shank. Bind the strands there about 1/4-inch behind their cut ends with plenty of tight thread-turns; keep the thread-collar fairly slim, but not too slim or the strands may slip free. (If you need to move the strands for better distribution, use only two light-tension thread-turns, tug the strands around under the thread, and then add the tight turns.)

16. Pull a few of the stub-ends of the strands up firmly and snip them off close to the shank—the ends should snap back small and neat. Keep pulling up the stub-ends of strands and trimming until they're all trimmed off.

17. Turn the hook upside down and bind on the other section of strands, and then trim off the stub-ends. You can hold the ends of the strands with your right-hand thumb and finger if that helps, as you work the bobbin by draping it repeatedly over the strands and reaching around for it with your left hand, if that helps. Now strands (still connected by the tabs at their ends) should encircle and sweep back over the body.

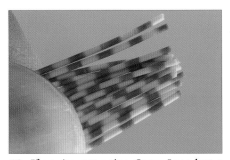

18. If you're not using Crazy Legs but a rubber-strand that comes free, in individual unattached strands, no problem—just gather the strands and pinch them into a sort of flat sheet, hold them flatly to the top of the shank and bind them, and then trim off their ends. And then do the same with more strands on the underside of the shank.

19. Wind on enough thread to cover the cut ends of the strands, whip finish the thread just behind the barbell eyes, trim the thread off.

Lightly stretch back one section of strands and trim off the tab-end. Draw back the other section and trim off its tab-end. The ends of the strands should reach between one third to two thirds down the tail.

20. Draw the rubber-strands back along the body and wind a few spirals of stout (0.025-inch works) lead-substitute wire over them to hold them back out of your way.

Coat the thread around the barbell eyes and the short thread collar over the rubber-strand with head cement or epoxy glue.

THE HARE WATERPUP

Dave Whitlock sat tying at a table, on the front of which lay an aquarium. It was the big annual fly-fishing show for trade people, and the company that produced Dave's fly patterns was showing him off. A stick lay across the corners of the aquarium; some tippet hung from one end of the stick and ran down into the water to a fly I recognized as Dave's Hare Waterpup.

"What's the stick for?" I asked.

"You work the fly with it, see what you can make it do."

I raised the stick; the fly jerked up its broad head. I lowered the stick to watch the head dip. Each movement of the neatly sculpted hair head sent a soft wave down the length of the tail, and with each wave the tail swelled and flattened. The fly was so lively in part due to its supple tail and weighted head, and in part because my hand was shaking—I was, after all, standing before a fly-fishing luminary.

The Hare Waterpup gets its "Hare" from its rabbit-strip back and tail (a hare is a rabbit, in case you didn't know). "Waterpup" is Dave's reference to a young waterdog salamander, which the Hare Waterpup imitates, and which Dave says "bass love to eat." Dave may well be the first to describe a young waterdog as a "waterpup."

But the Hare Waterpup imitates not just waterdogs but all kinds of long, flattened creatures—in the letter he sent me, Dave mentions sculpin, tiny catfish, and suckers, and says that these are only a few examples. He says also that the Waterpup is used for fishes other than bass—pike, stripers, muskellunge, walleye, snook, and

brown and brook trout. But I think of it mainly as a largemouth-bass fly, though I can imagine it has a place with smallmouth too.

Dave ties his Waterpup in three sizes—2 1/2 inches long on a size-4 hook, 3 1/2 inches on a size-1/0, and 5 to 6 inches on a 3/0. He always ties it on a traditional Atlantic-salmon-fly hook with an upturned loop eye.

There are three basic color combinations Dave likes for his Waterpup, though he suggests you match whatever colors your bass are used to seeing in their prey. These are his combinations: (1) black with a cream belly, (2) purple and chartreuse with a white belly, and (3) the "natural" version listed below.

Here is what Dave's letter said about how to fish his Hare Waterpup: "This Waterpup fly is very soft with wonderful underwater movement regardless of how slowly it is fished. It's most effective when fished near or on the bottom with almost no movement. The unweighted version can be fished on or near the surface day or night with excellent results. It can also be deadly when fished with a 2-4 ft. leader and a fast sinking or sink tip line in deep water where it dives and swims just off the bottom structure, slowly diving and rising with each pull and pause of the line. The weighted version sinks almost vertically and can either swim along or be jigged with a 7 to 9 ft. leader and floating fly line. It performs equally well in still and flowing waters."

That says it.

HARE WATERPUP NATURAL

Hook: Heavy wire, atlantic salmon, sizes 4, 1/0, and 3/0.

Thread: For everything but the hair head: white 3/0. For the head: any hair-flaring thread in a color to blend with the head's color.

Weight (optional): Lead wire, two thirds the diameter of the hook's shank.

Rib: Fine copper wire.

Body: Cream or pale-yellow long-fiber dubbing (Dave lists rabbit fur, Partridge SLF, and Antron dubbing).

Back and Tail: A strip of tanned natural rabbit hide with fur (a Zonker strip).

Throat: Cream or pale-yellow Flashabou dubbing (I couldn't find this, so I use Lite Brite) over dyed-red rabbit fur.

Pectoral Fins: Two short dyed-yellow saddle hackles.

Skirt: The tips of the first hair-bunches.

Head: Light-tan deer hair underneath, olive and black deer hair on top.

Eyes: Solid-plastic, or hollow-plastic with free pupils.

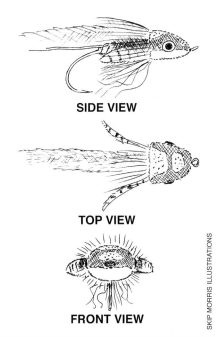

SIDE VIEW

TOP VIEW

FRONT VIEW

1. Start the 3/0 thread two thirds up the shank. Bind the end of the snag-guard monofilament there, and then spiral the thread tightly down the shank and mono to the bend. (I'm assuming you want a snag guard; if you don't, just start the thread at the bend.) At the bend, bind some copper wire atop the shank. If you want the Hare Waterpup to sink easily, add 6 to 20 turns of lead wire up the rear two thirds of the shank. (There are several ways to fish both the weighted and unweighted Hare Water-pup; they are described in the beginning of this section.) Dub a full, tapered body up two thirds of the shank.

2. Cut a strip of rabbit hide, with fur, about 1/8-inch to 3/16-inch wide (depending on hook size). The strip should be about 2 1/2 hook-shanks in length. Or just use a pre-cut Zonker strip (not a *crosscut* strip). Trim the fur back slightly from the end of the hide, the end from which the fur slopes; then bind that end atop the front of the *body* (not atop the shank).

3. Wet only the fur that is directly over the hook's shank with tap water. Pull the rabbit strip forward to hang. Take a half turn of the wire up the body, in an open spiral. Pull the rabbit strip back and down onto the body under light tension. With the tip of your bodkin, part the fur and then wind the wire through that part, over the hide. Continue parting the fur and spiraling the wire forward in four to six ribs up the body and rabbit strip. The tight ribs should secure the rabbit strip firmly atop the body. Bind the wire at the front of the body with tight thread-turns. Trim the wire.

4. Tease out the fur body to rough fullness using a bodkin.

5. Cut two wide, short saddle hackles to shank length. Bind one on each side of the front of the *body* (not on the shank).

6. Invert the hook in your vise. At the front of the body, extending back over the belly, bind on a short tuft of dyed-red rabbit fur. The tips of the fur should reach no further back than the end of the body. You can snip the fur from a skin or from a precut Zonker strip, or use a substitute.

7. Over the rabbit tuft, bind a tuft of Flashabou Dubbing (or Lite Brite). Trim the Flashabou dubbing to slightly longer than the rabbit-fur tuft. You can add a bit of head cement or epoxy glue around the front of the body to help secure all this, if you wish (with good ventilation, and then let the adhesive fully cure before working further on the fly—it's most efficient to add the adhesive to a bunch of fly-bodies at once, then complete all the flies later).

8. Advance the thread to just ahead of the body and whip finish it; then trim it. Start some hair-flaring thread over the whip finish. Return the hook to upright in your vise. Comb and stack some pale deer hair. Bind the hair lightly over the shank; then rotate the hair to the hook's underside (see "Stacking Hair Colors" in section III, "Flaring and Shaping Hair"). The hair's tips should reach to the rear end of the body and not beyond.

9. Comb and stack a bunch of black deer hair, about two thirds the size of the pale bunch. Bind the black hair tightly atop the hook over the pale hair. Mash down the black hair with your thumb. The tips of the black hair should be even with the tips of the pale deer.

10. Atop the black hair, bind a stacked bunch of olive hair, same size as the black. The tips of the olive hair should be even with the tips of the black.

11. Pull back the butts of all the hair—keep the pale hair below, the black and olive on top—and advance the thread. Stack the same series of hair colors again and compress that hair back into the first bunches. This may be enough hair for a small hook; a larger hook may require one or even two more sections of flared hair. In any case, flare and compress hair only to the hook's eye (or slightly short of the eye, if you included a snag guard).

12. Trim the head to a rounded, tapered shape, flattened top and bottom, as shown in the illustrations. Leave most of the stacked hair-tips intact, but trim away enough tips to at least partially expose the hackle pectoral fins. You can also trim away most of the pale hair-tips, to expose the belly if you like.

13. Complete the snag guard, if you included one. Trim out eye sockets and glue on the eyes (see "Eyes, Hollow or Solid-Plastic, Glueing on" in section IV, "More Techniques"). Add head cement to the whip finish behind the hook's eye.

THE SHINEABOU SUNFISH

A friend who is a really sharp fly-fisher once told me he didn't think largemouth bass eat many bluegill. "Why not?" I asked. "There're usually lots of bluegill in bass lakes, and just one makes a big meal."

He paused, looked calmly straight into my eyes, and then spoke a single word: "Spines."

I understood—bluegill have stiff, pointed spines mixed into their fins. Almost anyone who's caught a few bluegill has felt the prick of those spines. I imagined trying to swallow a whole spiky, thrashing bluegill and felt my mouth hurt. So I wrote bluegill off my list as bass feed. But I mentally logged my usual trace of skepticism.

In late afternoon the following summer I was fishing a tiny bass-bluegill pond, one oval acre behind an earthen dam. I'd never found a decent bass in it, but I'd caught some good bluegill. For some reason the fish were down. I tied on an SMP (a fly you'll read about soon), let its weighted eyes carry it down, and then worked it slowly just off the bottom. Every couple of casts I'd feel the slow resistance of pond weed or the thump of a bluegill.

The last arc of the sun dropped finally behind a ridge, rimming its jagged outline with soft, yellow light. The bluegill came right up with that; the pond soon dimpled with their activity. So I put up a little Skip's Fusion Bug, a floating hair bug, and cast it across the open water near the dam to the edge of the weeds. I let it lie quiet, then made it dive and float back up again and again, and caught bluegill after bluegill, mostly small ones but with an occasional good one to keep me wondering.

When the ridge had receded into night and the pond's face had gone black, a good bluegill swirled on my bug and panicked at the hook's bite. Then came a heavy swirl and a deep throb down the rod—a big bass had taken my bluegill. I struck hard, praying the bluegill was lightly hooked and that the fly would snap from its mouth into the bass. The rod throbbing another moment; then the bluegill popped from the water and skimmed flat-sided across its surface, the little bug still pinned all too solidly to its jaw.

I didn't know why or how, but I knew then that despite the spines, bass eat bluegill. In retrospect, it's hard to imagine bass getting on *without* eating things that poke or bite or pinch. Smallmouth and large-mouth bass eat biting dragonfly nymphs and pinching crayfish, and likely all kinds of biting, pinching things. So why not bluegill that poke?

After that I took a second look at Jimmy Nix's Shineabou Sunfish. I had seen plenty of flies with feathers lashed atop a body by a rib, Matuka style, but I'd never seen the effect doubled—feathers both atop and beneath the body—and was impressed at how well this suggested the flattened bulge of a bluegill. But the Shineabou Sunfish's heavy barbell eyes were mounted atop the shank, and that concerned me. I knew how well that same placement of such eyes inverts the Clouser Deep Minnow, and that's fine because the Clouser is designed to ride upside down. But I couldn't imagine an upside-down bluegill looking plausible to a bass. So I tied a few Jimmy's way; then I tied a few with the lead eyes beneath the shank. Tied my way, the flies looked wrong—the eyes were too low. Then I trimmed down the tops of the heads, left a little extra underneath, and the flies looked fine.

In the end, Jimmy's way worked. All that steel in the wide-gape bass-bug hook keeps everything upright, just as long as the retrieve isn't too quick.

But I still tie my Shineabous with their eyes beneath the shank. I think I can retrieve them faster that way, without concern that the fly will turn over. But my whole approach to fly fishing is neurotic, so perhaps this eye-business is just more of that.

I've found that, regardless of how the eyes are mounted, some Shineabous turn on their sides, especially on a fast retrieve. The best defense I've come up with is to make sure the eyes are centered on the hook's shank, their weight evenly distributed to the sides. But maybe Shineabous are supposed to turn; maybe this makes them look vulnerable or injured. My homework remains unfinished.

The tying instructions below for the Shineabou describe, as usual, the way I personally tie it.

As for how to fish the Shineabou, I usually work it around shallow cover, a slow swim, an occasional brief pause to let its lead eyes dip its head. If that's not working, I may scoot the fly along in darts—that's always a reasonable tactic with most bass flies; it can spark a bass into reacting out of pure instinct.

SHINEABOU SUNFISH

Hook: Heavy wire, short shank (standard bass-bug hook), a total hook-length of about 1 1/4 to 1 3/4 inches.
Thread: Olive, green, or brown 3/0.
Eyes: Lead (or lead-substitute) barbell eyes, yellow with black pupils.
Rib: Copper wire, fine to medium.
Body: Olive Antron dubbing (or another sparkling dubbing).
Double Matuka Wing: Grizzly hen saddle hackle dyed olive (the best feathers I've found for this wing are called "soft hackle," broad, dense, webby rooster hackle).
Gills: Red marabou.
Over-Wing: Olive marabou.
Head: Olive, orange, and black wool.

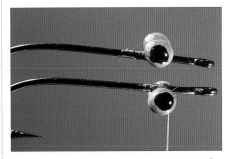

1. Start the thread three quarters up the shank and secure a pair of painted lead (or lead-substitute) barbell eyes there with tight crisscrossed thread-turns. Jimmy prefers the eyes mounted over the shank, like the top eyes in the photograph. I prefer them mounted below, like the lower set. (See "Eyes, Barbell, Binding on" in section IV, "More Techniques.")

2. If you want a snag guard (see section II, "Snag Guards"), secure the end of some monofilament two thirds of the way up the shank; then spiral the thread down shank and mono to the bend, and then partway down the bend. Snag guard or no, bind the end of some copper wire at the bend, atop the shank—really lock on the wire with tight turns of thread. Dub a thick, tapered body up two thirds of the shank.

3. Cup a matched pair of webby saddle hackles together, tips evened. Strip the fibers from their base. The remaining unstripped part of the feathers should equal the full length of the hook. Cup, even, and strip a second pair of saddles.

4. Hold a set of the hackles over the body. The fibered part of the hackles should start directly over the front of the body; the hackles' tips should project off the bend. Strip the fibers from the *underside* of the hackles. This stripped area should equal the body's length. Do the same with the other hackle-set, but strip the *top* of this set.

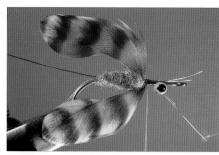

5. At the front of the body, atop the hook, bind the set of hackles whose *undersides* were stripped further than their tops. Bind the other set below the shank at the front of the body so that, like the top set, the stripped stems face the body. Add plenty of tight thread-turns; then trim the stems.

6. Wind the wire one-half turn to the bottom of the shank. Draw the underside hackles up to the body, one feather on each side of the hook's bend. With a bodkin or hatpin, part the hackle fibers, where the copper wire meets them. Wind the wire through the parted fibers. Release the wire—its memory will keep it curled around the hackles' stems.

7. Draw the top pair of hackles down to the body; the tips of these hackles should lie outside the tips of the lower pair. Part their fibers as you did with the lower hackles' fibers, and then wind the wire through the part. Continue this process, parting and winding through all the hackles, to the front of the body. Now the hackles should be locked in place with four to six wire ribs. Bind the wire under tight thread-turns; trim the wire.

8. Bind two tufts of red marabou at the front of the body, so each extends along a side of the body, for gills. The tufts should reach about three quarters down the body. (Wetting the marabou makes it easiest to handle.) Trim off the butts of the marabou.

9. Bind a good-size bunch of olive marabou atop the shank, at the front of the body, extending back over the body. The tips of the marabou should just reach the tips of the hackles. Trim off the marabou's butts.

10. Cut a smallish bunch of dyed-orange lamb's wool from the hide, and then trim straight across the wool's very tips, leaving a mix of natural and cut tips. Bind the wool under the shank; its tips should extend back about halfway down the body. The butts of the wool should extend well forward. The orange should stay beneath the shank and the red marabou gills.

11. Trim the tips of a bunch of olive wool as you trimmed the tips of the orange. This bunch should be about as thick as the orange bunch. Bind it *atop* the shank, tips again reaching about halfway down the body and forward off the hook's eye.

12. Draw the butts of all the wool firmly back, olive over the top and orange underneath, and pull the thread sharply forward. Add a few tight thread-turns at the front of the wool. Same procedure as basic deer-hair flaring.

13. Cut another bunch of olive wool. The bunch should be about equal in density to the first bunches of olive and orange wool combined. Hold the wool bunch lightly in front of the hook's eye, the wool's fibers in line with the hook's shank. Push the wool straight back over the hook's eye, down the shank, around the barbell eyes, and well down the body. Hold the wool secure as you take a turn of thread around it and the shank; then pull the thread tight. The wool should be secured *behind* the barbell eyes and back against the front of the first bunches of wool. Add a few tight thread-turns.

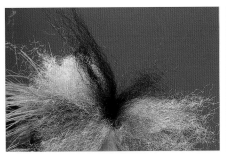

14. Push the wool down flat on top, so the wool divides on both sides of the thread-turns that bind it. Spread a small amount of black wool over the top half of the olive wool. Wind on and tighten another turn of thread. Add a couple of tight thread-turns; then draw the wool back and secure it as you did the first bunches. No need to compress the wool as you would hair—the wool spreads and covers naturally. Actually, you don't want the wool too dense or the fly will tend to float. (The title of this section is *"Sinking Flies"*…remember?)

15. Advance the thread to the front of the barbell eyes. Continue adding bunches of olive wool topped by black wool to the hook's eye just as you added these latest bunches. Add at least three sections with three toppings of black wool in all. Whip finish the thread, and then trim it.

16. Trim the head to broad and blunt when viewed from the side, thin when viewed from the top. Trim the rear of the wool enough to expose the red-marabou gills, and make the head thin enough to expose the barbell eyes. A razor blade won't work here, but scissors are very efficient with wool. Complete the snag guard, if you included one, and complete the fly with a whip finish and head cement.

VII. DIVERS

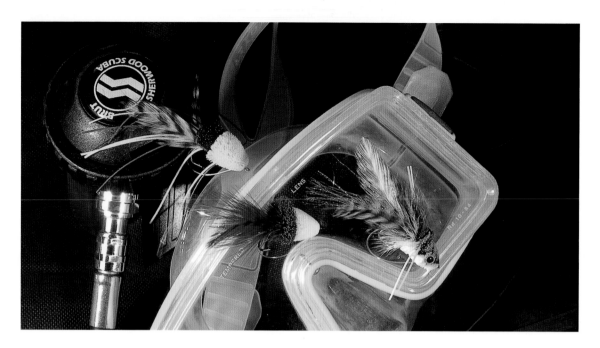

Most divers are wonderfully versatile. Because they float and because most can make chugs and pops and gurgles as they submerge, they can be worked as though they were standard hair bugs. But with a steady draw on the leader, rather than a short tug, divers will slide quietly under the surface. Often I have fished a diver strictly as I would a hair bug for an hour, then fished that same fly as a true diver for the next hour. Even more often I have fished a diver back and forth as hair bug, diver, and then hair bug again, freely switching as often as the fishing seemed to dictate. Sometimes there are clear reasons for fishing a diver one way or the other—over a shallow weed bed a dive could mean a fouled fly, but a dive down even a few inches alongside a dock could catch the eye of a bass tucked back in shadow.

What a diver won't do is skim or skip across the water's surface, but that's its only real limitation, a trade for its valuable ability to dive. Plenty of other flies skim and skip. A diver also won't shimmy or wobble like a plug with a lip as it swims—and few bass flies will—though many divers can come close to such movements if retrieved artfully.

For largemouth bass a deadly strategy is to make the diver struggle a bit, perhaps with a chug or pop—or, for subtlety, a gurgle—then pause, then make it dive and dart along underwater on a twitchy retrieve. The struggling suggests that whatever creature the fly represents is weakened or disoriented, the pause suggests that creature is catching its wind, and the dive suggests that it's fleeing to safety. It's that fleeing that makes bass pounce like the predators they are. But of course it makes more sense to grab the creature before it flees, and they often do.

Smallmouth bass take divers too, though my hands-on experience with these flies is greatest with largemouth. So I turned to Harry Murray's book *Fly-Fishing Techniques for Smallmouth Bass*. In it, Murray says he gets "upstream of the edges of grassbeds" and casts a Dahlberg Diver (one of the three divers we'll tie in this section) downstream to "about a foot from the edges of the grass." He then strips the fly in, to make it dive. After the dive, he pauses "to allow it to come back to the surface." He says he can hook several bass along a weed-bed by working a Dahlberg down along it in this fashion. He says he also enjoys "experimenting with it using every action I can think of in many different parts of the river." I'm sure his comments apply to all diving bass flies. Harry's known nationwide as an authority on smallmouth fly fishing, so his word on this Dahlbergs-for-smallmouth business ought to satisfy about anybody.

The divers in this section are all similar in shape—that's what makes them dive. Regardless of the particular design, there will be a plane (though it may be a curving plane) angling from the hook's eye back along the top of the body or head. If this plane takes a steep angle, the fly will dive sharply but stay shallow; if the plane takes a long, low angle, the fly will dive gradually, but deeper.

Divers have really caught on among bass anglers, and for good reasons, the main one being the flies' versatility. If I were forced to chose a single fly for all my surface and near-surface fishing for bass, that fly would surely be a diver.

TYING DIFFICULTY
(1 is easy; 5 is difficult)

Dahlberg Diver	4
Skip's Fusion Bug	4
Dave's Diving Frog	5

THE DAHLBERG DIVER
(and The Umpqua Swimming Frog)

Larry Dahlberg's Dahlberg Diver has become for bass what the Woolly Bugger has become for nearly everything else—the first fly beginners think of, regardless of conditions, and the fly experienced anglers carry and use.

The pattern for the original Dahlberg Diver is listed in section XIII, "Additional Bass and Pan-Fish Flies," and it's a shocker—a drab natural-tan-brown deer-hair body towing a long hank of brilliant gold Flashabou. Of course it's caught a great many bass, but since fly fishers are generally more concerned with what *they* like than with what fish prefer, the Dahlberg Diver has changed. Its alarming tail is seldom seen anymore, and its plain undyed deer-hair brown is usually replaced by dyed purple or green or yellow.

The Dahlberg Diver I'll describe here is a composite, a blend of ideas from a number of sources, and about the way I normally tie it. But don't hesitate to play with variations on this fly. You might even try the original—Larry knows bass, so I'm sure the design works.

Fish the Dahlberg Diver as you would any other diving bass fly, as described in the introduction to divers at the beginning of this section. Tie it in whatever colors and with whatever tail and proportions suit you...everyone else does.

DAHLBERG DIVER

Hook: Heavy wire, wide gape (bass-bug hook), a total hook-length of about 1 to 1 3/4 inches.
Thread: For the tail: 3/0 in a color to blend with the tail. For the hair-collar and body: any hair-flaring thread in a color to compliment or blend with the colors of the collar and body.
Tail: Flashabou inside two marabou plumes inside two sets of hackles.
Skirt: The stacked tips of the body-hair.
Diving Collar: Same hair as in the body.
Body: Deer, elk, or antelope hair.

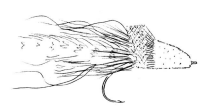

SIDE VIEW

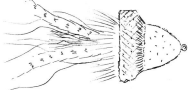

TOP VIEW

FRONT VIEW

SKIP MORRIS ILLUSTRATIONS

1. If you want to include a snag guard, start the 3/0 thread at the center of the shank, bind one end of the monofilament there, wind the thread down mono and shank to partway down the bend, and then back up to the rear of the shank (see section II, "Snag Guards"). If you don't want a snag guard, just start the thread at the bend. In either case, double three to five strands of Flashabou over the thread, secure them slightly ahead of the bend, and then wind the thread back over the doubled strands.

2. Wet two marabou plumes, measure each to a full hook-length, and then bind one on each side of the Flashabou, at the bend. Trim the butts of the marabou and bind them. I like to bind the butts of the marabou clear up to mid-shank and then trim them there, but you can trim them shorter if you prefer.

3. Bind on two sets of hackles (two or three hackles in each set) just back from mid-bend. A set can be tied in on each side of the shank or both can be bound atop the shank (see "Hackle Tail" in section IV, "More Techniques"). The hackle-sets should have evened tips and should project from where they're bound on 1 1/2 to 2 full hook-lengths. The sets should curve away from one another.

6. Comb, flare, and compress bunches of hair to the eye (or just back from it if you included a snag guard). Unlike the first two bunches of hair, these final bunches of hair should be well-distributed around the shank. Half hitch the thread a few times and trim it.

9. Trim the collar hair to a half-fan, projecting above and out to the sides of the tapered body. Avoid cutting the stacked hair-tips (remember how you stacked the first bunch of hair and bound it on with its tips back?). Usually the collar projects out from the rear of the body at least half the body's thickness; in other words, if the body is 1/2-inch-thick where it meets the collar, the collar will extend *at least* 1/4 inch beyond the body. But there are no hard rules regarding this, so feel free to experiment.

4. Whip finish the 3/0 thread just ahead of mid-shank (and just ahead of the snag-guard mono, if there is any) and trim it. Start some hair-flaring thread over the whip finish. Cut, comb, and stack a large bunch of deer or elk hair. Bind the bunch at mid-shank (just in front of the snag guard, if you included one). Try to keep the hair entirely, or at least mostly, *atop* the shank. The stacked hair-tips should extend back part way down the tail. Make certain the butts are left long enough to form the diving collar—the tips can be any modest length. Pull the hair back and advance the thread in enough turns to keep the thread from slipping.

7. Trim the front hair flat and close to the hook underneath and tapered on the top and sides. The result should be a sort of half-cone, as shown in the photos and illustrations. On the top and sides, stop cutting when you reach those first two bunches of hair that were kept atop the shank—that hair will soon become the collar. You can trim all the way back underneath the hook.

10. Trim the Flashabou to tail-length or slightly beyond. Complete the snag guard (if you included one), and add head cement to the whip finish at the hook's eye. Some tiers stiffen the hair diving-collar with head cement or Flexament.

5. Bind another hair-bunch, of normal size, just ahead of the first. Point the butts back on this bunch. This second bunch needn't be stacked but should also be kept atop the shank. Compress the second bunch back into the first.

8. Push back the collar hair with your scissors as you trim the rear of the tapered body. Or you can simply cut back to the collar hairs with the razor blade or scissors, if you're not concerned about having a neat color line between body and collar (a color line is only an issue if you used different colors of hair for the collar and body, as on the finished fly at the start of this chapter).

11. This is the Umpqua Swimming Frog, a close cousin to the Dahlberg Diver. The biggest difference is that the Umpqua Swimming Frog has a flange or rim of hair along the lower edges of its body. This flange alters the fly's diving motion—each approach has its believers. Try both.

THE SKIP'S FUSION BUG AND ELK HAIR

The Skip's Fusion Bug makes the best possible use of its two most significant materials—deer hair and foam-sheeting. The front end of a diving fly should ride low, should keep its nose slightly submerged, ready for a downward lunge; once the deer-hair (or elk-hair or antelope-hair) body of the Fusion Bug soaks up enough water it will hold its nose down consistently. Yet no matter how sodden the deer becomes, the foam holds everything afloat. The foam's lightness and buoyancy also tend to right the fly should it land upside down or on its side.

As with many bass flies, the Skip's Fusion Bug can be whatever color or colors you think your bass will like; the flies pictured are only two of many possible color combinations. The tail can also be whatever you like—hackles, a fur strip, Krystal Flash, or combinations of these and others. The rubber-strand legs can be omitted, but I do prefer them on all but pan-fish-size hooks.

I chose to tie the Fusion bug here with elk hair, though I tie it with deer more often than elk. Tying with elk, I can show you how it differs from deer, and how to make it behave. Elk *is* different from deer.

Although I created the Skip's Fusion Bug for largemouth and smallmouth bass, it's among my favorite flies for bluegill (and other pan fishes). For them I tie it on hooks as small as size 14, although a size-10 dry-fly hook is my bluegill-standard. In tying the Skip's Fusion Bug on small hooks I often simplify the tail, and always omit the legs.

There is nothing special about the ways in which the Skip's Fusion Bug is fished; just fish it as you would any other diver, as I describe at the beginning of this section.

SKIP'S FUSION BUG

Hook: For bass: heavy wire, short shank (bass-bug hook), a total hook-length of about 1 to 1 3/4 inches. For pan fish: standard dry fly (or a small bass-bug hook), sizes 14 to 8.

Thread: For the tail and collar: 3/0 in a color to blend with the tail. For the body: a heavy hair-spinning thread in a color to blend with the color of the body.

Tail: Three to five rubber-strands of colors to match or blend with those of the body and collar. Outside the strands, two sets of wide webby grizzly hackles of two or three hackles per set, hackle color to match or blend with the color of the body.

Diving Collar and Collar Support: Soft, buoyant closed-cell-foam sheeting. Two layers of foam can be used on the largest hooks. Any bass color. My current favorite foam for Skip's Fusion Bugs on large hooks is Evasote, about 1/8 inch thick; for small hooks I like foam sheeting about 1/16-inch thick. Buy colored foam to suit, or color white or pale foam with a permanent marking pen)

Legs: A pair of rubber-strands, two colors—one to match the body, one to match the collar.

Body: Any flaring hair of any bass-fly color.

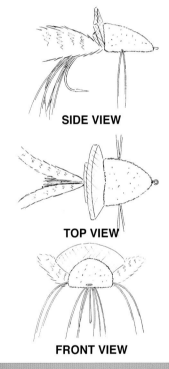

SIDE VIEW

TOP VIEW

FRONT VIEW

SKIP MORRIS ILLUSTRATIONS

1. Start the 3/0 thread at the bend. If you want a snag guard, bind on some mono-filament, its end directly over the hook's point (see section II, "Snag Guards"). Bind three to five lengths of rubber-strand atop the shank with a few tight thread-turns, just ahead of the bend. The strands should be bound at their centers.

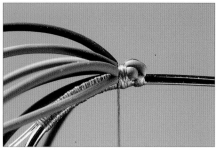

2. Pull the strands back off the bend, slightly upwards, and hold them there. Work thread-turns back to the bend. Add a few tight turns *at* the bend to really secure the strands. Now the strands should be secured and should be trailing off the bend.

3. Match four or six broad hackles into two sets. Each set should be even at the tips with the feathers cupped together. Pinch the sets together, tips evened, the sets curving apart. Snip the hackle-sets at their base to one length, about 1 1/2 to 2 full hook-lengths. Do *not* strip the fibers from the base of the cut hackles. Bind a hackle-set along each side of the rubber-strands as shown. (Or simply bind on the hackles all together, atop the rubber-strands; see "Hackle Tail" in section IV, "More Techniques.")

4. Whip finish and cut the 3/0 thread (just ahead of the end of the mono, if you added mono, directly over the hook's point if you didn't), and then start the hair-flaring thread over that whip finish. Wind about a 1/16-inch-long layer of thread forward; then wind halfway back over this first layer. Snip a small triangle out of foam sheeting. The triangle should be longer than it is wide. Snip off the long point of the triangle to blunt. Secure the triangle about one third up from its blunt tip at its center with a few firm (not tight) thread-turns. The large end of the triangle should project forward, towards the hook's eye; the small, blunt end should project rearwards. (The triangle is tipped to the side so you can best see it; it should be directly on top.)

5. Advance the thread tightly up the shank about 1/8 inch forward (toward the hook's eye) of the first thread-layers, the layers atop which the foam was bound. Wind the thread back (towards the bend) halfway over this newest layer of thread. Snip another triangle out of the foam sheeting; this one should be at least as long as the entire hook. Its sides should all be one length—or its top can be even wider than its sides.

Trim its point to blunt. Bend back the front (large end) of the *small* triangle.

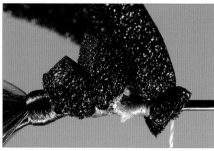

6. Still holding back the small triangle, lay the large foam-triangle back against it. Now the front of the *small* triangle should be pushing forward against the *large* foam-triangle. The blunt-cut tip of the large foam-triangle should face forward. Secure the large foam-triangle by its blunt end with lots of firm thread-turns. Only two thread-turns have been added here so that the orientation of the triangles to one another and to the hook is apparent; I usually add at least five turns of thread.

7. This photograph shows the large foam-triangle bound on, and above it, an identical triangle seen along its flat.

CREATING THE FOAM COLLAR

1. Wind the thread forward in a short layer, and then wind it back to the center of that layer. Bind a small foam triangle there near its blunt-cut end. The wide end of the triangle should project forward, towards the hook's eye.

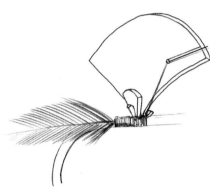

2. Wind another layer of thread forward and then wind the thread back over itself to its center of this layer. Draw back the large end of the small foam-triangle and bind a larger foam-triangle atop the thread layers. This larger triangle should have a blunt tip, and that tip should point forward, towards the hook's eye.

8. You should now have a fan or half-circle foam-collar standing upright and tipping slightly back, supported there by the first, smaller triangle of foam.

Wind the thread up the shank a bit. Flare a bunch of hair just forward of the foam-collar, *at least* 1/16 inch out in front of the foam-collar. (The closer this hair is to the foam-collar, the more that collar will tip back. Flare a second bunch of hair and compress it back into the first. Add two or three sets of long rubber-strands (see "Rubber-Strand Legs" in section IV, "More Techniques").

9. Flare and compress hair, one bunch after another, up the shank to the hook's eye (or just short of the eye if you included a snag guard). Look closely at the elk hair in the photo above—it's coarse, compared with deer hair. What you can't see is that it's also stiffer than deer. Actually, elk can be almost as soft as deer, but that's rare. I can seldom compress elk as densely as I can deer. Elk's biggest advantages are its toughness and it's stubborn buoyancy. In flared-hair bass flies, though, deer's buoyancy and durability do the job.

10. While working the rubber-strands out of harm's way (see section III, "Flaring and Shaping Hair"), trim the body to a shape that is flat beneath, rounded and tapered on top, as shown in the illustrations and photos.

Because elk hair is tougher than deer you'll probably notice more resistance to the scissors when you trim elk, and if you use a razor blade, you'll find that a worn blade is useless.

11. Trim the foam-collar to length. (Round its pointed edges, if you wish.) I usually trim the collar to project up and out from the body at least half the body's thickness. In other words, if the body is 1/2 inch thick (top to bottom, not side to side) at the foam collar, I'll trim the collar so that it projects *at least* 1/4 inch beyond the body. But feel free to experiment with this. A long collar seems to make a bigger chug when you jerk the bug forward than does a smaller one, but too large a collar can make the fly too bulky for a fish to take in, especially with little Skip's Fusion Bugs for such pan fishes as the bluegill with tiny mouths.

12. Draw the rubber-strands lightly up and trim them to length. Cut them at least a full hook-length from the shank (up to twice that length). Complete the snag guard, if there is one, whip finish and trim the thread, and add head cement to the whip finish. It's always wise to invert the finished Skip's Fusion Bug and work some epoxy (low-odor epoxy, with good ventilation) around where the foam-triangles are bound on.

It probably just took you 10 to 20 minutes to complete your first Skip's Fusion Bug. Congratulations! It took me three years.

13. Here is a Skip's Fusion Bug with no rubber-strand legs, a pale underside, a two-color back, and solid-plastic eyes; beneath it another that is simplified and tied pan-fish size.

THE DAVE'S DIVING FROG

The other two diving flies in this section each have a half-round body and a substantial diving collar; the Dave's Diving Frog has neither. But the approach Dave Whitlock used for this pattern makes sense. Once the flattened, arched top of the Dave's Diving Frog's body catches under the water's surface, the fly simply *must* dive. The short collar creates not a pop or a chug, really, but a gurgle and a few bubbles, which strike me as the most plausible result of a frog's plunge under water.

As with most of the flies in this book (and in all my books, in fact), I've incorporated my tying style into this one. If you want to tie the Dave's Diving Frog exactly as Dave does, I suggest you get Dave's video, "Fly Tying Bass Flies."

There are four color-variations for this fly: the white-belly version presented here, the orange-belly version (with a fluorescent-green and black back), the yellow-belly version (with a fluorescent-green, olive, and black back), and the gray-belly version (with a yellow, gold, and brown back). Sure, any hair fly with this many colors squeezed into it will be tricky and a bit time-consuming to tie, but who wouldn't enjoy seeing a few in his or her boxes, or tying one onto a tippet and tossing it out among the lily pads now and then?

Dave likes to fish any diving fly on a sink-tip line. The line really tugs the fly under on a draw; then the buoyant fly rises back up. It's a sensible approach that brings out the most in the fly's diving action. But you can just fish the Dave's Frog Diver on a floating line; simply make the fly dive, swim, and rest as you think a real frog might.

DAVE'S DIVING FROG, WHITE-BELLY VERSION

Hook: Heavy wire, short shank (bass-bug hook), a total hook-length of about 1 to 1 3/4 inches.
Thread: White or yellow 3/0 for the tail; white or yellow hair-flaring thread for the body.
Tail: Pearl Krystal Flash inside two sets of hackles, each set containing a white hackle inside a barred-yellow inside a barred green.
Skirt: One barred-yellow hackle. Around the hackle, the stacked tips of the first bunch of body-hair.
Diving Collar and Body: White flared hair for the belly; olive over black over yellow flared hair for the back.
Front Legs: One rubber-strand of each of the following colors: yellow, black, and white. I often vary the color and number of legs.
Eyes: Solid plastic, black pupil inside yellow or orange.

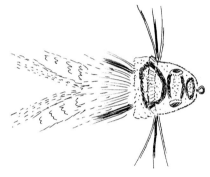

TOP VIEW

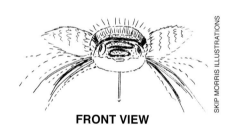

FRONT VIEW

SKIP MORRIS ILLUSTRATIONS

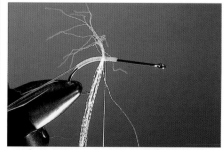

1. If you want a snag guard, bind some monofilament atop the hook's shank and down its bend with 3/0 thread (see section II, "Snag Guards"); if you don't want a snag-guard, just start the thread at the hook's bend. Lightly bind 15 to 20 strands of Krystal Flash atop the shank, slightly ahead of the bend. Add tight crisscrossed turns of thread to set the strands out at a right angle to the shank.

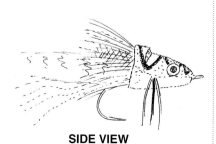

SIDE VIEW

2. Pull the Krystal Flash firmly back; then add a few tight thread-turns at the front of the strands to hold them back in a wide "V", as shown.

3. Hold a hackle-set (white inside grizzly-dyed-yellow inside grizzly-dyed-green) against one side of the shank, at the bend. Bind the set to the side of the shank with tight thread-turns. Bind on the other set on the other side of the shank. The sets should curve apart, their tips should be even, and they should be about 1 1/2 times the full length of the hook. (See "Hackle Tail" in section IV, "More Techniques.")

4. Strip the base of a big yellow-grizzly hackle and bind it to the shank, about 1/8 inch forward of where the hackle-sets are bound on. The hackle should project out to the side and forward towards the hook's eye; the butt of the hackle should project back. Trim off the hackle's butt.

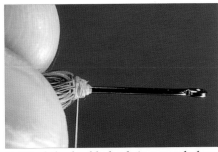

5. Wind the hackle back in several close, tight turns; secure the hackle's tip with a couple of thread-turns; and then spiral the thread *forward* through the hackle fibers. Trim out the hackle's tip. Draw the fibers firmly back using the triangle (see "Triangle" in section I, "Essential Techniques"), and then add tight thread-turns against their front. The result: the fibers now tip steeply back.

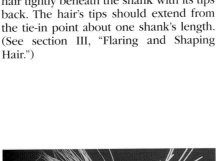

6. Comb and stack a modest-size bunch of white deer hair. Slightly up the shank from the hackle, about 1/8 inch, bind the hair tightly beneath the shank with its tips back. The hair's tips should extend from the tie-in point about one shank's length. (See section III, "Flaring and Shaping Hair.")

7. Comb and stack a bunch of yellow deer, about two thirds the size of the white bunch. Bind the yellow hair tightly atop the white. The yellow hair's tips should be even with the tips of the white hair.

8. Press down especially hard on the yellow hair, over the thread-turns binding it, to flatten and spread the hair. This is part of Dave's method for forcing the yellow hair to the sides, so that little of it winds up on top. The other part of his method lies in how the hair is pulled back.

9. Atop the yellow hair, bind a bunch of stacked black hair about two thirds as thick as the yellow-hair bunch, tips even with the tips of the yellow.

10. Atop the black hair, a bunch of stacked olive hair, tips even with the tips of the black. The olive-hair bunch should be about the same size as the *yellow-hair bunch*. Dave adds yet another hair bunch, a small bit of black atop the olive, but it's optional and I've skipped it here.

11. Draw back the hair and add a few tight thread-turns. Pull the yellow hairs down to the sides and stroke them hard until they stay there.

12. Bind on two or three rubber-strand legs, a mix of any of the following colors: yellow, orange, green, white, and black. (See "Rubber-Strand Legs" in section IV, "More Techniques.")

13. Bind another bunch of white hair underneath; then yellow atop it, as before. After mashing down the yellow, work its rear ends to the sides of the previous hair-bunch. (The yellow hair needn't be perfectly distributed to the sides; in fact a bit of yellow on top looks good.) Add black hair atop the yellow and olive atop that, as before. This hair needn't be stacked.

Continue adding sections of hair in the color-sequence of the first hair-section up to the hook's eye (just back from the eye, if you included a snag guard). Whip finish the thread or make three half hitches. Trim the thread.

14. Trim the body as shown in the illustration at the beginning of this chapter and the photos—blunt and slightly tapered when viewed from the top, trimmed fairly close beneath, a modest taper when viewed from the side, and slightly rounded when viewed from the front. The body should appear somewhat flattened on top. Trim all the white hair back to the stacked hair-tips, but no farther. All the hair above the white should stop at a rough hair-collar.

15. Trim the collar neat and short. It should blend into the body along the sides, tapering off completely down where it reaches the white hair.

16. Trim the Krystal Flash to the same length as the tail-hackles. Trim the rubber-strands so that they extend from the *body* (not the shank) a distance slightly greater than the shank's length. Trim out an eye-socket on each side of the body and glue on the eyes. (See "Eyes, Hollow or Solid-Plastic, Glueing on" in section IV, "More Techniques.")

VIII. INSECTS AND CRAYFISH

Flies modeled on insects and crayfish cling to the ragged shirt-tail of respectability for largemouth bass, but they lie right in the pocket for smallmouth. That's because largemouth eat insects and crayfish only on occasion while smallmouth eat them all the time. In fact, smallmouth eat these creatures so often that the mostly insect-suggesting Strymph and the crayfish-imitating Skip's Quivering Cray are first-rate fly choices for a smallmouth river almost any time and under almost any conditions.

Personally, I consider insect-imitations for largemouth bass underrated. It's not that a bulging Messinger Bucktail Frog or a dodging, billowing Skip's Hover Bug aren't the sort of flies you should normally prefer, because they are; it's just that, once on a while, largemouth want nothing but a dragonfly adult. You'll understand when you read about the Betts' Foam Dragon.

TYING DIFFICULTY	
(1 is easy; 5 is difficult)	
Strymph	3
Skip's Quivering Cray	3
Betts' Foam Dragon	4

THE STRYMPH

Harry Murray, author of *Fly Fishing for Smallmouth Bass* and *Fly-Fishing Techniques for Smallmouth Bass*, created the Strymph. The man clearly knows smallmouth, and he's come to trust his Strymph as a deadly smallmouth fly, so it makes perfect sense that we should trust it too.

Harry treats the Strymph as both a streamer and a nymph. In *Fly Fishing for Smallmouth Bass* he lists all kinds of creatures smallmouth eat and that can be imitated by Strymphs of various colors and sizes. Among them: hellgrammites, dragonfly nymphs, leeches, damselfly nymphs, tadpoles, sculpin—and that's less than half the list.

The Black Strymph came first, but Harry now ties his Strymph in olive and cream and suggests that nearly any natural color may be useful. His simple rule is that the tail and body should about match in color, and the hackle's color and markings should "blend" with that color. After looking at some Strymphs Harry tied, I take "blend" to mean at least similar to the body and tail color.

I assume that the name "Strymph" is a combination of the words "streamer" and "nymph" since Murray fishes his fly as both. Exactly *how* it's fished depends, of course, on what it's supposed to imitate at the moment. If you want it to suggest a drifting stonefly nymph, let it ride freely with the current along the stream bed; to make it imitate a minnow, make it swim like one. Want your Strymph to look like a dragonfly nymph? Then retrieve it in darts close to the riverbed. The Strymph, in various colors and sizes, suggests so many things upon which smallmouth feed that you could make a hobby out of finding ways to fish it.

STRYMPH

Hook: Heavy wire, 2X or 3X long, sizes 8 to 2.
Thread: Three-ought of a color to match the color of the body.
Weight: Lead or lead-substitute wire.
Tail: Ostrich herl matching the color of the body.
Body: Black, olive, or cream rabbit fur.
Hackle: Speckled hen saddle (hen back) similar to the color of the body and tail.

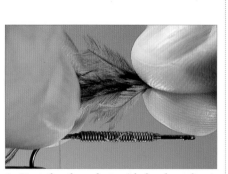

1. Start the thread at mid-shank and spiral it back to the bend. Wind a layer of lead wire over most of the shank, but terminate the wire well short of the hook's eye and bend. Secure the lead with tight thread-turns. Murray suggests using lead-wire that is about the same diameter as the hook's wire.

Find a stretch of ostrich herls, still on the feather, that are full and long-fibered. Stroke 15 to 20 herls out to an angle that roughly evens their tips. Snip the herls free at their bases; hold the herls firmly to keep their tips even. *Tear* (not cut) off the very tips of the herl bunch with your thumbnail.

2. Measure, and then bind the herls atop the shank at the hook's bend, using the pinch (see "Pinch" in section I, "Essential Techniques"). The herls should extend from the bend a distance roughly equal to the length of the hook's shank. Trim the herls' butts where they meet the lead.

3. Pull at least five inches of thread off the bobbin. Stroke tying wax along the thread, and then double it back to the shank creating a loop of thread, a "dubbing loop." Wind the working thread back over the ends of the thread-loop to secure it.

Wind the thread forward to just back from the eye. Hook a dubbing twister into the end of the thread-loop. Snip some rabbit fur from the hide—a "Zonker strip" or "crosscut rabbit strip" is a good source—and put it into the loop; an alternate approach: clamp the tips of the fur in a bulldog-clip (from an office-supply store), snip off the hide strip, slip the fur into the dubbing-loop as shown here, and open and remove the bulldog-clip. (See "Zonker Strip" in section IV, "More Techniques.")

4. Keep constant light tension on the dubbing-loop. Pinch its sides together as you tease the fur to distribute it along the loop. The strands of fur should lie at roughly a right angle to the thread. Try to position the fibers so that the thread holds them at their centers—this may take a few very light pushes or taps.

Spin the dubbing twister until the fur is tightly locked into the loop. If you're using a dubbing *whirl*, try draping the bare tip of the dubbing loop over your finger and *then* giving the dubbing whirl a spin.

5. Wind the fur-loop up the shank, drawing the fur back after each turn is added.

6. Secure the thread loop just back from the eye by binding it with tight thread-turns. Trim off the end of the loop. Whip finish the thread.

Remove the hook from your vise and trim the body to a taper as shown. You can work around the hanging thread or trim it and restart it later, whichever you prefer.

7. Pluck a hen-saddle (also called "hen back") hackle from the skin. Strip the hackle of its fuzz along the base of the stem. The remaining fibers shouldn't be much longer than half the length of the shank. Bind the hackle on by its stem, just behind the hook's eye. The body of the feather should now project forward, off the eye. Wind the thread *back* in close, tight turns along stem and hook's shank to the front of the fur-body.

8. Trim off the hackle stem's butt. Wind the hackle back in two close turns. Wind the thread over the tip of the hackle to secure it. Whisk your fingertip around the hackle fibers to make them separate. Spiral the thread *forward* through the hackle-fibers to the hook's eye.

9. Trim out the feather's tip. Stroke back the feather's fibers using the triangle (see "Triangle" in section I, "Essential Techniques"); then build and complete a thread head.

THE SKIP'S QUIVERING CRAY

In the original edition of *The Art of Tying the Bass Fly* I proudly unveiled a pattern I called the Skip's Dad (as in the slang term "crawdad") that had reliably convinced even the most belligerent smallmouth in Oregon's Umpqua River to take a bite. I'd drop the heavy fly onto rocky riverbed in lazy water, and then creep it only a half inch or so every few seconds. The bass would all but line up for it. Best of all, it was "sight fishing," the whole magnificent show of fish moving to fly in plain view. So, I had a deadly fly pattern for a fascinating method of fishing— what could go wrong?

I found out exactly what could go wrong a few years later when I courageously weaned myself off the addictive Umpqua and started fishing other smallmouth streams more often. In other rivers, it turned out, the Skip's Dad wasn't nearly as effective. It caught smallmouth, yes, but not with anything like the spell it cast over the Umpqua fish. So I set out to create a new crayfish pattern that did. I tried a hard back of plastic-sheeting; claws of various materials, some trimmed to shape and others of feathers or fur left natural; several types of fanned tails; various legs… The usual evolutionary process creeping unsteadily toward a fly's proper design.

The first thing I required of the fly was that it rode with its hook-point up—the low swimming and occasional riverbed bumping common with crayfish-fly retrieves would beg snag-ups if the point rode down. That was easily accomplished: I mounted heavy barbell eyes on the top of the hook, to flip it over.

My second requirement was lots of movement. I'd watched the legs and claws and antennae of alarmed crayfish trail suddenly like streamers behind the darting crustaceans, and then watched these appendages all swing loosely back out to resting position when the creature paused. So I worked with the claws first, wanting them supple enough to move, but not soft and lifeless either. In the end I'd found nothing better than the pheasant-tail-fiber claws from my old Skip's Dad. Further testing convinced me the antennae and legs were best made of springy rubber-strand.

The shell-like exoskeleton of a crayfish offers no real movement to suggest in a fly, other than the flipping tail. But whenever I tried a tail that doubled back under like a real crayfish tail pumping away, I got a fly that rode unnaturally on its side or, worse, turned upside down altogether—an obvious impostor. Besides, when a crayfish swims, it swims *fast*, a blur of motion, an impression. So I gave up fighting the laws of physics, abandoned the soft-tail idea, and compensated by making the thorax shaggy and lively. It's a good effect. (The completed fly above was tied with soft

dyed-rabbit fur for the abdomen; the fly tied in the steps to come uses slightly stiffer Arizona Sparkle Nymph Dubbing. Both are effective. Experiment.)

The barbell eyes gave me grief. They and their placement were crucial to the fly's performance, but they protruded unnaturally from the sides of the abdomen no matter how I tried to hide or disguise them with various tail designs. Then one day it struck me that the eyes swelled out right where the tail belonged and in a sort of tail-shape. So instead of camouflaging the barbell eyes, I emphasized them—they *became* the tail. It was easy once I saw the logic. I simply painted them to match the abdomen and suddenly their tail-shape seemed to blend naturally in.

A Skip's Quivering Cray whose abdomen and thorax dubbing includes brilliant Mylar strands seems particularly attractive to some smallmouth. You can skip the glitter by using a quiet dubbing such as plain dyed rabbit if you prefer, but I've caught heaps of smallmouth on glittering versions.

By now, after a long succession of experimental crayfish patterns and lots of time hunting smallmouth with them and with the final version you see here, I've had such consistent success with the Skip's Quivering Cray that I feel I've finally completed my quest: to create a crayfish-fly that's as good on other smallmouth rivers as the Skip's Dad is on the Umpqua.

I probably fish my Skip's Quivering Cray in tan more often than in olive or brown, but each color has its place. Smallmouth, in my experience, aren't usually sticklers about fly color, but if all the crayfish in your river are olive, then an olive crayfish-fly just makes good sense. Day in, day out I find it hard to beat a Skip's Quivering Cray on a size 6 hook. But if the smallmouth run only eight to ten inches—which is still big enough to pull hard and leap—I'll switch to size 8. Size 4 is for large fish.

In streams of modest size I use a full-floating line and toss the Skip's Quivering Cray upstream, let the fly drift and sink, and

then retrieve it with quick strips of the line separated by brief pauses. In big or deep rivers I use a sink-tip line. I've learned from my years of fishing trout lakes to keep the rod pointed straight down the line and the rod's tip down on the water; this way, with no slack in the line and the rod's soft tip-end unable to cushion the tug of a strike, I'll feel one immediately. That's important, because a smallmouth can grab a fly and spit it back out in a wink. It's hard to really understand the speed of this maneuver until you actually see it.

There are challenges here for your tying skills. Setting the claws properly and neatly and dubbing around them take some practice, as do setting the legs and working the dubbing and rib through them. But eventually, the Skip's Quivering Cray becomes pretty easy and quick at the vise.

I leave my Skip's Dads untouched in my boxes during most of my smallmouth fishing now, instead plucking out and tying Skip's Quivering Crays onto my tippets. A long and intimate association with the Skip's Quivering Cray and its ancestors, and all those smallmouth voting repeatedly for it with their strikes, have convinced me.

SKIP'S QUIVERING CRAY

Hook: Heavy wire, 2X (or 1X) long, down eye, sizes 8 to 4.

Thread: Three-ought in the abdomen's color.

Weight: Lead or lead-substitute barbell eyes. For size 8, 1/80-ounce "mini" (or 1/60- to1/50-ounce "extra small"); for size 6, 1/60- to 1/50-ounce (or 1/40- to 1/36-ounce "small"); for size 4, 1/40- to 1/36-ounce.

Antennae: Two doubled strands of dark (brown or black) fine rubber-strand.

Nose: A tuft of the thorax dubbing.

Eyes (optional): Heavy black monofilament melted on the ends or premade eyes on stalks.

Thorax: Tan, brown, or light- to medium-olive or green rabbit blended with fine Mylar strands (Angel hair or Lite Brite) in silver, pearl, and the general color of the rabbit. Or Arizona Sparkle Nymph Dubbing.

Claws: Pheasant-tail fibers, undyed or dyed to blend with the thorax's color.

Rib (optional): Medium-diameter natural-color copper wire (or any color you like).

Abdomen: Same dubbing as in the thorax.

Legs: Two doubled strands of medium-diameter rubber strand in a color similar to the color of the abdomen. I like rubber-strand with markings, even a little glitter.

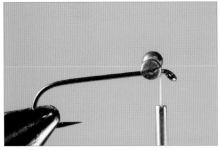

1. Bind the barbell eyes on *slightly* back from the hook's eye (see "Eyes, Barbell, Binding on" in section IV, "More Techniques").

2. Double two five-inch lengths of fine dark rubber-strand over the thread, bind them atop the shank right behind the barbell eyes. Hold the strands back and raised a little and bind them down the top of the shank to *slightly* (no more than 1/8 inch) down the bend. Mount the strands back out of your way in your material clip. Bind a clump of dubbing atop the strands slightly down the bend (no further than where the rubber-strands are bound), to project back a little over the strands. (If you want crayfish eyes on your fly, melt lengths of heavy black monofilament, such as Amnesia, to make little globes on stalks, or buy premade eyes, and then bind them on to extend out to the sides of the tuft of dubbing.)

3. Stroke wax down the thread, spin dubbing thickly and roughly onto the thread, and then dub a thick ball over the rear eighth of the shank (and over the thread windings going slightly down the bend). This will become the rear of the thorax.

4. Invert the hook in your vise. Stroke a bunch of pheasant fibers out from the stem to whatever angle evens their tips. For this size-6 hook, the section would lie along about one inch of the quill. Measure the fibers against the shank, and then bind them atop the shank right in front of the ball of dubbing, using the pinch (be careful not to poke yourself with the hook's point). The fiber-tips should extend back, from where they're bound, a full shank's length.

Bind a second bunch of fibers on, same amount, same length, terminating at the tips of first bunch. If you like the effect of thick claws, add a third bunch of fibers.

5. Hold the butts of the fibers lightly up and back, and spiral the thread up the shank to the barbell eyes. Lower the fibers and bind them just behind or over the stem of the eyes. Raise the butts of the pheasant-fibers and cut them off.

6. Spiral the thread tightly down the shank to the tips of the pheasant. Push the point of your bodkin (or closed scissor blades) straight down into the center of the pheasant-fiber tips, to divide them equally to the sides. Tug the two bunches of fibers firmly out to the sides, so they lie separated after you release them.

7. Wind crisscross turns of thread around the shank and between the fibers to secure them out to the sides.

8. Option: wind a few firm (but not fully tight) turns of thread around the base of one of the bunches of fibers, and then do the same with the other bunch. This will gather the fibers into neater groups. This can be a tricky step that's really about the fly's aesthetics, not its effectiveness. Bass don't know what claws are; the pheasant-fibers create an impression and complete the fly's form, neither of which need be exact.

9. Pinch the groups of fibers back so they form a "V" off the bend. Tug them up, so they angle upwards slightly (this will help the fly ride properly). Pinch the fibers back against the sides of the dubbing. Wind the thread back tightly—just a little—over the fibers' bases to secure their position. Don't wind the thread back more than a few close turns at most, or you'll angle the fiber-claws too far back. An option: after you pinch the fibers back and angle them upwards, just cover the bases of the fibers with turns of dubbing during the next step instead of binding the bases with bare thread.

10. Wax the thread and then spin dubbing roughly and heavily onto the thread. Stroke back the pheasant-fibers and pinch them down to hold them in place again. Dub the front half of the thorax right in front of the claws—try not to knock them out of position as you dub. (Option: make a dubbing loop as on pages 58 and 59 for the Strymph and slip a line of dubbing into the loop; build the rear half of the thorax, add the pheasant-fiber claws, and then complete the thorax with another dubbing loop. Makes a really full, fuzzy thorax.) Dub heavily to fill out the thorax, but not so heavily you block much of the hook's gape.

11. Bind the end of a length of copper wire along the top of the shank from the barbell eyes to front of thorax. (The fly fishes fine without this rib, so omit it if you like. But it does add quiet segmentation and a little extra durability to the abdomen.)

12. With the thread coming from the front of the thorax, double about a two-inch section of rubber-strand over the thread, slide it down the thread to the shank, and bind it firmly on one side of the shank with a few tight thread-turns wound all in one place. Cut another section of rubber-strand and bind it in this same manner on the other side of the shank. If the ends of the strands angling forward don't angle well out, hold them back firmly and add some tight thread-turns against the front of them.

13. Dub over the thread-bindings that hold the rubber-strand (trying not to knock the legs out of position as you do so). Pull back all the strands and dub right in front of them. Continue dubbing up the shank to the barbell eyes to make a stout and slightly tapered abdomen. Spin the dubbing tightly onto the thread and not too heavily so you build up a firm abdomen into which the wire rib won't sink and disappear entirely. To really compress the dubbing, try swiping a little wax onto your fingertip before spinning the dubbing around the thread. Because the dubbing is spun on thinly, you'll have to either build it back over itself repeatedly as you work up to the eyes, or make a layer of dubbing forward and then a layer back and then a third layer forward again, to get the abdomen up to size.

14. Wind the copper wire up the dubbed abdomen in five or six tight, equally spaced ribs. Be careful to avoid knocking the legs out of position as you work the wire around and perhaps through them. Bind the wire at the barbell eyes. (You can bind the wire and then double it back and bind it again, to really lock it down, if you like.) Cut off the end of the wire closely.

15. Wind the heavy thread all around the stem of the barbell eyes, covering any dubbing. Whip finish the thread right behind the hook's eye and cut it.

16. Pick out the dubbing all around the thorax to shaggy, using a bodkin or dubbing teaser or your closed scissor blades. Trim the underside of the thorax to flat.

17. Trim the rubber-strand legs to length—about the length of the hook's shank, or slightly longer or shorter if that suits your eye. Trim the rubber-strand antennae—the two that lie on the outside to a little longer than the entire hook and the two strands that lie inside those to about half that length.

18. Paint the barbell eyes a color similar to the color of the dubbing. Almost any kids' non-toxic paint will do: poster paint, acrylic, watercolor.

19. Once the paint is dry, coat the eyes and thread windings around the eyes with low-vapor epoxy glue (using good ventilation) and then turn the fly until the glue sets.

20. Here's the head of a Skip's Quivering Crayfish with the melted-monofilament eyes I mentioned in step #2. To humans, these eyes make a difference; to a smallmouth watching your crayfish fly darting away, the mono eyes almost certainly go unnoticed. Make and add the eyes, skip the eyes, your choice.

THE BETTS' FOAM DRAGON

It took me a little while to catch on too the importance of adult dragonflies in largemouth-bass fishing (about 20 years). I used to occasionally see afternoon largemouth splash at dragonfly adults that hovered too close to the water, or through some miscalculation in their daring, acrobatic flight tumbled onto it, and consider the event an anomaly. Thinking back, I realize now that there were sometimes lots of splashes and that when there were, I caught little. The connection seems obvious now. And that's about all the confession my self-esteem can handle.

Anyway, I eventually *did* figure it out, around 1990 I think, when my previously good fishing died as bass began slamming down the abundance of dragonflies that were performing their wild carnival in the shallows. You couldn't miss it, so, finally, I didn't miss it. I had no adult-dragonfly imitations and needed a break from Central Oregon's blazing high-desert sun anyway, so I spent that break wolfing down a dry sandwich and tying a couple of hastily designed patterns. The flies, cast to the shallows and gently twitched, worked just right—nearly every new pocket in the reeds yielded a swat from another bass. Cold fishing had turned hot. So I tied on a standard hair bug and worked it in the same sort of water in which I'd worked the dragon pattern. Twenty minutes later I'd managed only one or two timid strikes. I switched back to my dragonfly imitation and over the next 20 minutes watched six to eight bass smack the fly. It was one of those rare experiments in fly fishing whose results are decisive: clearly, the bass had no real interest in anything other than dragonflies, and were after dragonflies with a vengeance.

After that, I began working on a better pattern than the one I'd rushed together that searing day in the desert. During the process

I discovered John Betts's fly, tied a few, fished them for a season, and decided John had done the thing right. So I offer you an adult-dragon imitation that's reliably caught me dragon-feeding largemouth bass for the past 20 years: the Betts' Foam Dragon.

It's an old and honored law of fly fishing that an imitative fly must do as the natural does, and the key to applying this law to the Betts' Foam Dragon is subtlety: a few *tiny* twitches, an occasional one-inch nervous skid between pauses. To really hone your technique for working a Betts' Foam Dragon, find a real dragonfly caught on the water's surface and just…watch.

BETTS' FOAM DRAGON

Hook: Light to regular wire, short shank (bass-bug or short-shank dry-fly hook), a total hook-length of about 1 to 1 1/4 inches.

Thread: Green 3/0.

Legs: Three strands of 50-pound Dacron fly-line backing or round rubber-strand, colored with a marking pen.

Wings: White Ocean Hair or FisHair (#70 Denier). (John uses clear nylon jig hair, which looks great, but I can't find it.)

Abdomen: Buoyant foam sheeting about 1/8 inch thick (John uses 1/4-inch Evasote, but I don't know where he gets it, and the 1/8-inch works very well).

Thorax: Light-green or chartreuse Furry Foam.

Back: Two layers of 1/8-inch foam sheeting (John uses 3/8-inch Evasote, but I don't know where he gets this either; the doubled 1/8-inch works very well).

Eyes: Dressmaker's pins with black plastic heads.

1. Cut three lengths of white rubber-strand or Dacron backing, around three inches each. Color them with light-green and blue marking pens. Color one length green or blue, the other two lengths the other color.

Bind the lengths of rubber-strand atop the center of the shank with a couple of modestly tight thread-turns; the strands should be bound at their center.

The strands will now lie in line with the shank, so pull one end of the strand-bunch out to one side, the other end out to the other, and then secure them there with tight, crisscrossed thread-turns.

Fly-line backing is shown here. Rubber-strand was used for the completed fly at the beginning of this chapter.

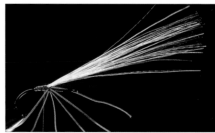

2. Right at the rear of the strand-legs, bind a bunch of white Ocean Hair or FisHair atop the shank. The hair should project off the hook's eye. Use lots of tight thread turns. It's hard to describe how much of the synthetic hair to use. I can only say that when it is later split into four wings, they should be sparse.

Ocean Hair is used here. Denier was used in the completed fly at the beginning of this section. (FisHair is considerably more supple the Ocean Hair.)

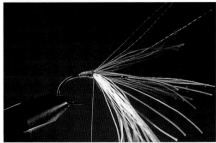

3. Split the wing-fibers into two equal bunches, out to the sides. This will require lots of tight thread-turns crisscrossed at the wings' center. Sometimes it helps to take a couple of turns around a wing's base, pull back on the thread, then secure the thread with a few turns around the shank. Spiral the thread to the bend.

4. Cut a slim (no wider than ¼-inch) strip from a sheet of white, buoyant closed-cell foam. Trim one end of the strip to a short point. With permanent marking pens (and good ventilation), color the strip blue on its top and sides, light-green on its underside.

Bind the strip atop the hook at the bend with lots of firm (not tight) thread-turns. The pointed end of the strip should extend from the bend about three full hook-lengths. The butt of the strip should extend forward past the hook's eye.

5. Draw back the butt of the foam strip and spiral the thread forward to just back from the hook's eye. Lower the foam and bind it there. Trim off the front end of the foam closely.

6. Cut a very thin strip from a sheet of Furry Foam (about 3/16-inch wide). Bind the strip to the shank just behind the hook's eye, projecting forward over the eye. Spiral the thread firmly back over the foam and shank to the bend.

7. Wrap the Furry Foam to the bend in close turns. Secure it there with a few thread-turns and trim off its end.

8. Cut two strips of foam from the same white sheeting you used to make the abdomen; they should be about twice the width of the abdomen's strip. Cut the strips straight across at one end. At the bend, bind the two strips of foam atop the hook with several firm thread-turns, one strip atop the other (if you can find thick enough foam, use just one strip, as John does). The strips should be bound close to their squared ends, as shown. The bulk of the strips should project over the hook's eye.

9. Wind the thread forward in one or two tight spirals to the wings and legs. Divide one wing in half, draw the rear half and one or two leg-strands firmly back. Hold all this back along the shank, and then do the same on the other side. Push the foam strips back out of the way. Give the remaining wing-fibers and legs—the ones you're not holding back—a tug so that they angle forward. Build a short collar of tight thread-turns at the center of the split wing-fibers and legs; this collar divides the wings and separates the legs.

10. Wind the thread towards the hook's eye in just one tight spiral, to about halfway between the thread-collar and the eye. Note in this close-up that the wings are well divided and the legs splay out to the sides.

11. Pull the foam strips forward and down. Bind them there with firm thread-turns.

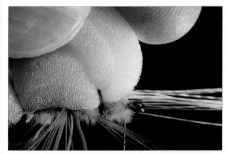

12. Pull back the front of the foam strips and wind the thread in another tight spiral to the hook's eye. Whip finish the thread there and trim it.

13. Trim the front of the foam strips straight across, at the rear of the hook's eye.

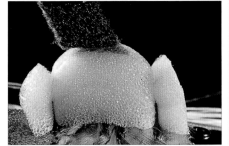

14. Color the foam-back with marking pens, blue on top, light-green on the sides, front, and underside.

15. Push a dressmaker's pin into each side of the foam face, as shown. I prefer to first cut the pins short, about 3/8-inch, and then smear a tiny bit of epoxy glue along the shaft of each pin. Make sure the pins go *inside* the thread-turns holding the foam in front.

16. Trim the wings to about the same length as the abdomen. Trim the legs; they should be no shorter than the hook's shank, no longer than the full length of the hook. Add head cement to the whip finish.

17. In the compartments of most fly boxes, the abdomen of a Betts' Foam Dragonfly often gets crushed and the wings misshapen. Here's the best solution I've found thus far—a big box with big compartments in which I cut a slot for the abdomens. I stack the flies, with each flipped the opposite direction of the one beneath it, as shown in the photo. The flies eventually shift around, but the slot helps.

CAROL ANN MORRIS

IX.PAN-FISH FLIES

It's easy to think of pan-fish flies simply as scaled-down flies for largemouth bass, and sometimes that would be right. Take the Fathead Diver—Jack Ellis freely admits that he modeled this stout, mousey, buoyant little pan-fish pattern after the Dahlberg Diver bass fly, and the similarities between the two are obvious. My SMP's relation to the Clouser Deep Minnow may not be as apparent, but I developed the SMP through the Clouser and both ride with their hooks inverted due to their heavy top-mounted eyes, and both thrust their wings back at their hook-points.

But the list of pan-fish flies that are *not* miniature versions of largemouth-bass flies is probably longer than the list of those that are. Example: the Sponge Spider, a pan-fish fly for subtle presentations that is unlike any bass fly I've ever seen. Same goes for the Woolly Worm and the McGinty and the Bumble McDougal and other pan-fish flies in this book; they just aren't anything like bass flies.

Not only are many of their flies different, but pan fishes and largemouth bass themselves are different too. In fact, these differences are what I love most about pan fishes—how they hold in different places than bass, take a fly differently, fight differently, and the rest. If pan fishes were effectively just little largemouth bass, a whole intriguing facet of fishing would be lost. But it gets even more interesting: pan fishes differ from one another, too. I've caught bluegill, crappie, pumpkinseed sunfish, green sunfish, white bass, rock bass, yellow perch and others and, to lesser and greater degrees, have found each species unique, each bringing its own challenges and delights.

Give pan fish an open mind and a chance to win you over. You'll likely find a fun and fascinating world of fishing in these minor warm-water players. And among the best parts of that world are the flies.

So if you want to describe the SMP as a "stubby little Clouser Deep Minnow" and the bluegill as "a round little largemouth bass that schools in the spring," go ahead, but it's a real stretch. And if you tell this to old-timers, expect to see skepticism—if not alarm—in their eyes.

TYING DIFFICULTY
(1 is easy; 5 is difficult)

Foam Spider	2
Carrot Nymph	3
SMP	3
Fathead Diver	4

THE FOAM SPIDER

Call it what you will—foam spider, sponge bug, sponge spider, foam blue-gill bug—it's still just a foam body, rubber-strands, a hook, and some thread to bind it all together. Bluegills and other pan fishes really go for a Foam Spider cast lightly or slapped down into their territory. Work a Foam Spider quietly—a tremble or twitch followed by a pause. It seems to be its subtlety that makes this fly effective—there is no popping or diving, no sparkling tinsel or flipping tail. The Foam Spider's plump body and gangly legs make an occasional little lurch to arouse a bluegill's curiosity, he investigates, he decides he's found something to eat, fish on!

I'll show you how to tie this fly with a premade foam body and how to make a body from foam sheeting. Either way, when pan fishes demand the subtle approach, the Foam Spider can be deadly.

FOAM SPIDER

Hook: Light wire, 1X long (dry-fly hook), sizes 14 to 8.
Thread: Three-ought in a color to match the color of the body.
Body: Soft, buoyant closed-cell foam sheeting or a premade foam-body.
Legs: Fine rubber-strand of a color to match or complement the color of the body.

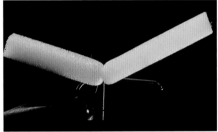

1. Start the thread just behind the hook's eye. Wind it in tight close turns to the bend. Cut a strip of closed-cell foam. The strip should be about as wide as the hook's gape. Bind the strip atop the hook at its bend with several *firm* (not tight; tight can cut the foam) thread-turns. The rear end of the foam should project off the bend at least one shank's length.

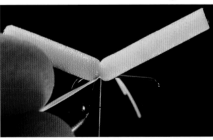

2. Loop a length of rubber-strand over the thread. Slide the strand to the foam body and secure it to one side with a few *tight* thread-turns. In the same manner, secure another length of rubber-strand to the other side of the body.

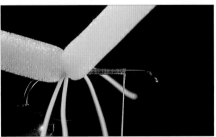

3. Lift the foam up and back. Spiral the thread tightly forward to about three quarters up the shank.

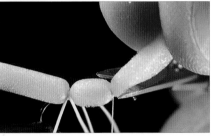

4. Lower the foam and secure it there with firm thread-turns. Add a Skip's Whip (see "Skip's Whip" in section IV, "More Techniques"), and then trim the thread. Trim the end of the foam projecting over the hook's eye straight across, directly over the rear of the eye.

5. Trim the foam projecting off the bend to shank-length, or slightly shorter. Trim both ends of the foam to rounded. Trim the rubber-strands to length, longish, about equal to the full length of the fly.

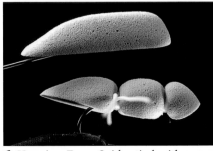

6. Here is a Foam Spider tied with a pre-made body; a sample body is suspended over it. Same tying steps, but you can let the foam reach slightly beyond the hook's eye if you wish.

THE CARROT NYMPH

The Carrot Nymph is an old-time Pacific Northwest trout fly I discovered in the mid-70s in Enos Bradner's book *Northwest Angling*, published in 1969. Back then I was trying to catch an occasional college class when I wasn't fishing—living on campus and paying my own tuition and living costs by playing music on weekends and through the summer freed me from my parents' suspicious looks. Not that I blamed them—I was a sucker for a real fishing day, still and cloudy, and when one appeared I was often dreamily driving one old clunker or another to some bass lake or trout stream, and they knew it. Actually, about any day there wasn't a windstorm was fair game and they knew that too. My instructors seemed confounded at how my grades improved when the rivers and lakes iced over in winter. Winters pulled my Ds up to Cs and my Cs up to Bs which hoisted my yearly average just above the expulsion level. I should have been grateful for winters just because they kept me in college, but instead I saw them mainly as a fishing obstacle.

One of the greatest threats to my attendance record was a popular gravel-pit pond of about two acres lying in dust and sagebrush just inside the city limits of the little college town. I pestered its healthy bluegill population with all sorts of flies but settled eventually on a size-12 Carrot Nymph as my standard there simply because the fly kept hooking me fish. In the spring I could catch bluegill on that pond from sunrise clear through sunset using the Carrot, which would wipe out an entire day of classes.

One day on the pond, while I was missing an English history class, the Carrot put me into a largemouth bass of at least three pounds. He took it quietly, panicked at the sting of the hook, and then towed me and my tiny boat in circles for a minute or two before the hook let go. When the fly came back I turned it by the tippet before my curious eyes and felt a whole new respect. Largemouth bass—especially the big ones—can become remarkably canny feeders when the fishing pressure is high and the water is small, as on the pond, and that three-pounder must have seen hundreds of flies and lures before he fell for my waving little orange nymph. The Carrot's caught me other bass, but for every bass there were a few dozen pan fish. So to me, it's still really a pan-fish fly.

But not to Bradner, the man who introduced me to the pattern. In *Northwest*

Angling he describes the Carrot Nymph as a "taker on cutthroats and brook trout in small lakes, beaver ponds, or sloughs." He gives no suggestion of what trout take it to be. He says only that "the 'live' action of the hackle fibers as the fly is stripped through the water usually produces a strike." Fair enough. Too bad he never gave it a chance with pan fish though—that live action produces strikes from them too.

There's nothing magical of course about the Carrot's particular blend of shape, colors, and materials. Add wings, change the body to yellow or white, add a tail and omit the gold tag, even tie the body short on a long-shank hook that you can use like a lever to help you free the fly from the tiny mouth of a bluegill—the fly will still catch pan fish. It will catch them because they see it simply as something alive and edible, not at all in the precise way a trout sees a cream and yellowy Light Cahill Parachute as another mayfly dun during a hatch.

So play with the Carrot Nymph if you wish, but remember that it's got a lot going for it just as it stands—a stout sparkling body, a winking tag of tinsel, waving insect-leg fibers of speckled partridge... Personally, I'll tie the Carrot pretty much as Bradner presented it (with the occasional obvious exception of a metal bead as its head), partly because I just like its bright and elegant original looks, but also because it's taken me lots of bluegill, including some specimens so big and plump they seemed to strain their own skins. And there were those large bass I mentioned...

But this isn't 1969, so I've made one change in the Carrot Nymph that was unavailable to Bradner: I use sparkling, shaggy synthetic dubbing for the body instead of the wool he lists in his book. Such dubbing wasn't around back then; in fact synthetic fly materials of any kind were rare. But twisted in a thread-loop this dubbing lends the Carrot a bright, corpulent

body that strikes me as almost irresistible to a bluegill or crappie or green sunfish.

I've long fished the Carrot Nymph just under the surface on a floating line, usually in the shallows, around cover, twitching life into its hackles and shaggy body. But I've done well with it down on a sinking line too. With a bead-head Carrot I fish a floating line and let the fly drop on its own weight; then I retrieve it slowly enough to keep it down one to several feet.

The Carrot is a handsome little nymph—or, arguably, wet fly, with its characteristic wet-fly tag and hackle-fiber collar—and, as I've proven to my own satisfaction over the past few decades, a solid fly for bluegill and other pan fishes. And, yes, as Bradner says, it can be good on trout, too.

CARROT NYMPH

Hook: Heavy wire, standard length to 1X long, sizes 14 to 8.
Thread: Black 8/0 or 6/0 (orange looks good too).
Tag: Flat gold tinsel.
Body: Bright-orange synthetic dubbing such as SLF, Antron dubbing, or Arizona Sparkle Nymph Dubbing in "Skip's October Caddis."
Hackle: A gray or brown partridge flank feather (I prefer the gray).

1. Start the thread at the bend. There, bind on some fine flat gold tinsel. Most flat Mylar tinsel has a silver side and a gold side. You can bind the tinsel on with its silver side up, and then fold the tinsel at its tie-in point as you begin wrapping it; or you can simply tie in the tinsel at an angle to the shank with the gold side up. Either way, you want the gold side showing for the finished tag. Wrap the tag as described in the illustrations. I like to use hackle pliers in wrapping the tinsel. The tag should reach three to five turns down the hook's bend.

WRAPPING A TAG

1. Wrap the tinsel down the hook's bend in a few close turns, each turn abutting the last, neither overlapping it nor leaving a gap next to it.

2. Wrap the tinsel back up the bend, again with each turn up against the last. When the tinsel reaches the thread, bind the end of the tinsel-end under tight thread-turns and trim it closely.

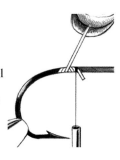

2. Pull down the bobbin until there are about ten inches of bare thread between it and the hook. Wax the thread.

3. Double the thread over a dubbing whirl (shown here) or a dubbing twister. Wind the end of the thread (the end coming from the bobbin) onto the hook's shank—the thread should now form a loop (called a "dubbing loop"), from which hangs the whirl or twister. Wind the thread toward the bend a bit to lock both ends of the loop in place. The loop should be secured at or just ahead of the bend. Spiral the thread forward to just behind the hook's eye.

4. Tease a small bunch of bright synthetic dubbing to an elongated triangle (shown is Partridge's SLF, but any bright dubbing is fine).

5. Open the thread loop and slip in the triangle of dubbing. The tip of the long dubbing-triangle should be near the hook; the length of the triangle should run along the length of the thread-loop. Pinch the sides of the loop together to hold the dubbing lightly inside the loop. Tease the dubbing so that it spreads out fairly evenly along the closed loop.

6. Spin the whirl or twister so that the loop of thread and dubbing twist together. If you are using a dubbing *whirl*, drape the end of the thread-loop over your finger; then spin the whirl like an inverted top. Try to wind the loop back so that the dubbing meets the shank right at the front of the tinsel tag. Wind the twisted thread-dubbing rope up the shank in close turns to slightly back from the eye. The dubbing in the loop will be shaggy, so it pays to stroke back each turn before adding the next. I often clamp the end of the dubbing loop into English hackle pliers for this work.

7. Secure the end of the dubbing loop with tight thread-turns; trim off the ends of the loop closely. Tease out the body-fibers to fullness with a bodkin. I like to remove the hook from the vise and trim the shaggy body to a taper or even a football shape; but leave the fibers long if you prefer. With care, this trimming can be done without cutting the thread. But whether or not you cut the thread before trimming the body, a half hitch at the front of the body is good insurance.

8. Strip the fluffy fibers from the base of a partridge feather and bind the feather by its stripped stem just behind the hook's eye, projecting off the eye. Wind the thread back in a few close tight turns over stem and shank to the front of the body, and then trim the stem. The fibers remaining at the base of the stripped stem can be as short as the hook's shank to nearly as long as the full length of the hook—a matter of personal preference.

9. Use hackle pliers to wind the feather back in two or three close turns to the front of the body. Hold the hackle pliers stationary as you spiral the thread *forward* through the hackle fibers to the eye. Let the bobbin hang. Trim out the feather's tip.

10. Use the triangle to stroke back all the feather fibers (see "Triangle" in section I, "Essential Techniques"). Build a tapered thread head, whip finish and trim the thread, add head cement to the head.

11. For a Carrot Nymph with a bead head, slip the bead up the shank to the hook's eye, with the small end of the hole in the bead forward, against the eye. Tie the fly as usual, but make sure you build the body right up against the rear of the bead. After winding the hackle, bind it and make a slim thread-collar behind the bead.

THE SMP

"SMP" is an acronym for "Skip Morris Pan Fish (fishfly)," and the name of a fly I designed for bluegill lying too deep for surface or near-surface flies. For that work it's been deadly. It has also proven effective on crappie, which I nearly always find holding down a few feet. And I've caught yellow perch, green sunfish, rock bass, and probably a few other species of sunfish on it. But even though I continue to catch largemouth and smallmouth bass occasionally on the SMP—and a friend considers it among his top smallmouth flies—I still have difficulty accepting it as a true bass fly. Of course, that could change…

The most effective approach I've found with the SMP is to let it sink to whatever depth finds the fish, and then draw it slowly and steadily back (though giving the fly an occasional shiver never hurts), rod tip down on the water to help me feel a strike. When I do feel one, I pull the hook home fast—bluegill, especially, can be quick to spit out a weighted fly. Sometimes I let the SMP sink for only a few seconds before working it; other times, I let it sink clear to the bottom first—it usually comes up without snagging.

The SMP resists snagging because it rides with its hook bend and point turned up. This is due to its bead-chain or lead-barbell eyes being mounted atop the shank; its down-eye hook; and its wing, which is mounted *beneath* the shank. I got the idea from Bob Clouser and Lefty Kreh's Clouser Deep Minnow.

As you'll see, there is a standard version of the SMP and what I call a "Short-Strike" version. I always carry both. Usually I start with the standard—it has the fullest, liveliest wing, which I believe catches the most attention from the fish. But if I'm missing strikes, which is usually because the fish are nipping only at the end of the wing, I switch to the Short-Strike SMP; its short wing leaves a bit of orange body—and hook—exposed at the rear of the fly, making it tough for a fish to nip anything without getting hooked.

The single-strand floss makes easy work of building up a body, and helps in really locking on the eyes—even a big bluegill has a tiny mouth, and working a fly out from deep inside

that mouth while the rest of the fish goes berserk can wrench at the metal eyes. Depending on how quickly you want or need the SMP to sink, you can use bead-chain eyes or lead-substitute dumbbell eyes. Colors are open. I've used all-black and a variety of lighter colors and combinations. All caught fish. (Still, I always start fishing with the reliable orange and yellow in the dressing below.) Try a silver-tinsel rib or nickel-plated eyes—they work too. A bit of Krystal Flash or Flashabou mixed into the wing and trimmed slightly beyond it is another option. This is a flexible fly pattern.

One word of caution: forceps can tear up the body and rib. Do use forceps—you'll often need to—but work them carefully. And in the instructions to come, I'll show you a couple of tricks for toughening that body and rib.

SMP, ORANGE-YELLOW

Hook: Light to heavy wire, standard length or 1X long (standard dry-fly or nymph hook), sizes 14 to 8.
Thread: Orange single-strand floss (or whatever color you wish). (I use Danville's Flat Waxed Nylon; some single-strand flosses are too thick and slippery for the SMP.)
Rib: Gold or silver oval tinsel or wire (or shiny synthetic dubbing with no rib).
Body: The same floss used as thread (or sparkling dubbing).
Eyes: Gold or silver bead-chain eyes or, to really sink the fly, lead or lead-substitute barbell eyes.
Wing: Orange marabou over yellow marabou (or whatever colors you wish).

---

1. Start the single-strand floss, as you would start thread, about three quarters up the shank. Bind the tinsel there using the pinch or a light turn (see "Pinch" and "Light Turn" in section I, "Essential Techniques"). Add a few more tight turns of floss. Lift the tinsel slightly above the shank under moderate tension. Wind the floss down shank and tinsel in abutting turns to *slightly* down the hook's bend.

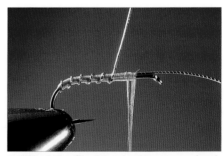

2. Wind the floss in abutting turns back up to its starting point (three quarters up the shank). Wind the tinsel up the body in six to ten open spirals to create the rib. Secure the tinsel with turns of floss, and then trim both of its ends at the three-quarters-up-the-shank point.

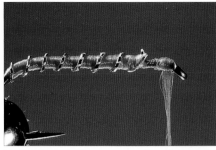

3. Build a little bump of a few tight turns of floss just behind the hook's eye (but not blocking the eye)—these turns will help keep the bead-chain eyes (or barbell eyes) in place as you bind them on.

4. Cut a pair of bead-chain eyes from the chain with tin snips, the insides of diagonal cutters, or the like (or use barbell eyes). Secure the eyes *tightly* with crisscrossed turns of floss. (See "Eyes, Barbell, Binding on" in section IV, "More Techniques.")

The eyes should be mounted no further forward than halfway between the hook's eye and the front of the body—this puts the eyes seven eighths up the shank. In fact, you may want the eyes only three quarters up the shank—this will make it easy to avoid covering the hook's eye with floss later.

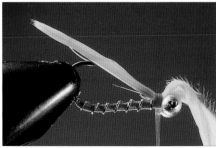

5. Invert the hook. Moisten a yellow marabou plume with tap water, and then bind it atop the shank, just behind the bead-chain eyes, with a few tight turns of floss. The marabou's tips should extend about a gape's width past the far edge of the hook's bend.

6. Bind an orange marabou plume over the yellow—same technique as for the yellow, same length. Trim the butts of both plumes *closely*. (Option: bind all the marabou with crisscrossed thread-turns *over the stem* of the eyes—this will keep the thread from working back and reducing the length of the wing and pushing it down.)

7. Cover the butts of the marabou with crisscrossed turns of floss between the bead-chain eyes, over their stem. Whip finish the floss crossways over the stem of the eyes, to leave as much wing unbound as possible—and trim its end. Add epoxy generously all around the thread-head between the bead-chain eyes (or barbell eyes).

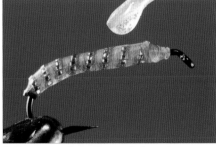

8. Forceps, when you work them to remove the fly from a pan-fish jaw, can cut the tinsel rib of an SMP. But you can really toughen the fly's body by coating it with clear, hard epoxy glue. The easy way to accomplish this is to tie a few SMP bodies, each with their thread (single-strand floss or flat waxed nylon, that is) half hitched and cut. Coat the bodies thinly (with good ventilation), and stick the hooks in an electric rotating wheel made specifically for curing flies with head cement (or in a board you flip over regularly). The next day, after the epoxy is hard, start the flat waxed nylon, bind on the eyes, and complete the fly. Epoxy or no, a bit of care when extracting the fly from a fish counts for a lot.

9. Another way to toughen the body of the SMP is to build it with sparkling synthetic dubbing—Antron dubbing, SLF, Arzona Sparkle Nymph Dubbing, Ice Dub… Just dub onto the flat waxed nylon.

10. The Short-Strike SMP begins with a long-shank hook, 3X or 4X long. Wind the floss fully halfway down the bend. Bind on the wing exactly as you would for the regular SMP, but the wing must terminate right at the end of the body.

This black Short-Strike SMP has a bit of Krystal Flash in the wing. Two strands of Krystal Flash were doubled over the thread and secured over the first marabou plume, then covered with the second. Flashabou or Angel Hair or Lite Brite in the wing are other options.

THE FATHEAD DIVER

In *The Sunfishes, A Fly Fishing Journey of Discovery*, author Jack Ellis describes his Fathead Diver pan-fish fly as "a very small Dahlberg Diver." Other than the tail on his fly, which is simpler and different from the tails on most Dahlberg variations, I'd say he's right.

While it may indeed be just another Dahlberg Diver, the Fathead Diver does have one unique feature: a snag guard uncommonly small and of unusual design. When I first saw this pan-fish snag guard, I was skeptical. I knew that most pan fishes have little mouths—so little that they've always seemed to have trouble enough getting a plump size-10 fly into those mouths without the added bulk of a snag guard. I figured too that a fly with a snag guard would sail free from the typical sipping takes of most pan fishes without coming even close to sinking the hook's point home. After all, largemouth bass, for whom snag guards were designed, clamp their broad, deep jaws around the things they eat—a whole different story from the timid workings of a bluegill's little mouth. So, based on my seasoned judgment and impeccable instincts, I wrote off Ellis's pan-fish snag guard and ignored it for a full year.

Eventually, curiosity drove me to tie a few Fathead Divers with exactly the snag-guard design Ellis describes in his book and prove, yet again, that I can be impressively wrong. The contraption worked.

In an article in *American Angler* magazine, Ellis describes a snag guard of 0.012-inch Maxima, but in *The Sunfishes, A Fly Fishing Journey of Discovery* he describes a snag guard of "Mason 8# (.012)." Same diameters, but the Maxima is the softer of the two, seems to do fine at avoiding snags, and is my first choice (but once you've read section II, "Snag Guards," you'll see that my fear of too-stiff snag guards borders on obsessive,

which may explain my preference for the Maxima. The Mason is probably just fine.)

In *The Sunfishes*, Jack describes three patterns for his Fathead Diver: the standard version below; a shad version with cream or pale-yellow marabou and pearl Flashabou over yellow kip-tail for a tail, and a cream or pale-yellow body and collar; and a frog version with grizzly hackles over chartreuse kip-tail for a tail, a chartreuse hair collar, and a cream or pale-yellow body. Jack avoids size-A rod-winding thread for flaring the hair in his diver; I prefer size-A for the fly and that's what I'll show you in the tying photos. But there's no right or wrong about this; as with many tying choices, it's personal.

The Fathead Diver does its work very well; I've convinced myself of that. Of course it is, as Jack himself freely admits, nothing new, just a couple of twists on an already established fly. Still, a little Dahlberg Diver with a little snag guard for pan fishes...good idea.

FATHEAD DIVER

Hook: Regular to heavy wire, short shank to 1X long (a little bass-bug or stout dry-fly hook), sizes 10 and 8.
Thread: Red 3/0 for the snag guard and tail; white or gray size-A rod-thread for the collar and body hair (Jack prefers 6/0 and 3/0).
Snag Guard: Mason or Maxima monofilament of 0.012-inch diameter. (A snag guard is optional.)
Tail: Squirrel tail under red marabou under brown marabou.
Skirt: The stacked tips of the first bunch of collar-hair.
Collar: Natural deer hair.
Body: Natural deer hair.

1. Start the 3/0 thread on the shank, directly over the hook's point; then bind on the end of the snag-guard monofilament, also directly over the point. Wind tight thread-turns to the bend—*do not wind thread down the bend as you normally would for a snag guard.* (A snag guard here is optional, as usual.) Bind a small bunch of squirrel tail atop the mono. Trim the hair's butts closely. The squirrel can be stacked, if you wish, and should project back 1 to 1 1/2 shank-lengths from where it is bound.

2. Bind a bunch of red marabou over the squirrel; then bind a bunch of brown marabou over the red. Trim the marabou's butts closely. Use only small amounts of marabou. The marabou should extend back beyond the tips of the squirrel a distance about equal to the width of the hook's gape, or slightly further. Here, I moistened the marabou with tap water before binding it on—this really makes fluffy marabou easy to control.

3. Whip finish the thread slightly ahead of the tail, trim the thread, and start some size-A rod-winding thread over the whip finish. Cut, comb, and stack a modest-size bunch of deer hair. Hold the hair-bunch atop the shank and take two light thread-turns around it. Hold the hair firmly in place and then pull the thread tight. The tips of the hair should end slightly ahead of the tips of the squirrel.

4. Secure another modest-size bunch of deer hair in front of the first; again, it should stay mostly atop the hook. This bunch needn't be stacked. Compress this second bunch back into the first.

5. Flare or spin and compress hair to just back from the hook's eye (or right up to the eye, if you skipped the snag guard). Whip finish the thread (or add three half hitches) and then cut its end.

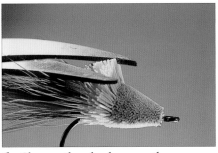

6. Shape the body exactly as you would for a Dahlberg Diver (see "The Dahlberg Diver," section VII, "Divers"). Trim the collar as you would for a Dahlberg.

7. Start the 3/0 thread at the hook's eye. Bring the monofilament down and forward, just outside the hook's bend, and then up through its eye. Adjust the mono snag guard to slightly undersize; then bind it to the *underside* of the *shank* with a few *light* thread-turns. Trim its end at the hook's eye.

8. Slowly and carefully pull the mono back until its end is under the shank, right at the rear of the hook's eye. The snag-guard loop should now look slightly oversize for the hook; use the photographs as a guide. Add some tight thread-turns to lock the loop in place, whip finish the thread, trim its end, and add head cement to the whip finish.

Just so you're not confused by these instructions: you didn't double the end of the mono back and bind it as usual for a snag guard because if you did, there won't be enough room remaining in the eye to accept a tippet.

Jack coats the hair-collar with head cement. I don't. Your choice.

X. BASS-FLY MATERIALS

All the flies you've learned to tie up to this point amount to a pretty exhaustive exposition of fly-tying materials as they're used in bass flies. You've learned to flare and trim wool and deer hair into lifelike shapes with pale bellies topped with striped and spotted backs; to bind on barbell eyes; to make wings and tails of marabou, buck tail, and hackle; and much more. You can work wonders with so many natural and synthetic fibers and feathers and components and such, and now it's time to take a closer look at these raw elements, to really understand them so you can choose and handle them even better.

A few general considerations. Note which materials are especially buoyant, as they make sense in floating bass flies. And note which ones are heavy or absorb water as these make sense in sinking flies. But remember that there are other qualities of tying materials—softness, for motion in the water (marabou and rabbit); brilliance (Flashabou and tinsel); bulk (deer hair and wool)—that may prove more important in a particular fly design than buoyancy or the lack of it. And the routine use of flared hair in flies for bass makes an understanding of that hair critical for the bass-fly tier (that's you).

CEMENTS

I'm a big believer in epoxy glue for fly tying—but don't confuse epoxy glue with epoxy *finish*, which is used in making fly rods and often releases strong vapors that are dangerous to breathe. For that matter, many epoxy glues also release nasty vapors

that can hurt you. So I work with low-vapor epoxies and I work with them *outdoors in a cross breeze,* so I never breathe or even smell the vapors. The specific low-vapor epoxy I'm using right now is Devcon 2-Ton Crystal Clear Epoxy.

I prefer a fairly slow-curing epoxy (the Devcon cures in 30 minutes) so I really have some time to work with it after I mix it up. And that's what you do with epoxy: mix it. Epoxy glue comes in two syrupy components, A and B, and you mix equal amounts of each to start the cure. I just squeeze out two puddles that look about equal, on the glossy paper of a magazine or on a plastic lid for a plastic tub that contained margarine or such, and then mix the components thoroughly together using a round toothpick. I use the toothpick (or a bodkin) to apply the epoxy.

Epoxy glue sets up *strong*—it really locks fly parts in place and makes thread heads glossy and tough.

To keep flared-deer-hair parts of flies from rotating on the hook's shank, I hold the fly upside down and run a line of epoxy up the underside of the trimmed hair, right over the shank, and then hit the epoxy with the hot air from a hand-held hair dryer. The epoxy sinks right in and grips the hair and shank.

"Dave's Flexament," developed by Dave Whitlock (whose name appears throughout this book), is a liquid, and consequently saturates materials better than epoxy can (although epoxy blasted with that hair dryer I mentioned comes close). Flexament can be used to stiffen materials, such as hair and feathers, yet this stiffness is rubbery, flexible. Dave feeds small amounts of Flexament into many of his flared-hair flies to make them fleshy.

There is the matter of glueing eyes to flared-hair bodies—common practice in tying bass flies. Dave Whitlock uses a pliant glue called Goop. Joe Messinger Jr. (of Messinger Bucktail Frog fame) uses plastic-cements, such as Duco. I use partly cured epoxy glue.

Plain old head cement from a fly shop has served fly tiers for decades. It's mainly used for securing thread heads and finishing knots on trout flies. There are all sorts of head cements, some basically clear fingernail polish, some newer ones non-toxic.

With all glues and head cements read the warnings that come with them and heed those warnings.

WAXES

There are soft and hard tying waxes. Each type has its supporters, but I prefer soft wax. Sliding wax along thread makes thread sticky, so natural or synthetic dubbing fibers will adhere and go on easily. I don't normally bother with wax unless the dubbing is coarse, such as squirrel or goat. (See "Dubbing" in section I, "Essential Techniques").

LEAD

To the fly tier, lead offers one valuable property: weight. So lead is used in sinking flies simply to get them down. Lead wire wound around a hook's shank once accounted for nearly all the weight added to nymphs and streamers, but that's changed—barbell eyes, bead-chain eyes, bead heads, and cone heads, made of lead or environmentally kinder metals, can do this same work while providing a chromey gleam or a suggestion of real eyes. Heavy bead-chain or barbell eyes, mounted atop the right hook, can make a fly ride point up, to avoid snagging on boulders or sunken wood.

TINSELS AND WIRES AND SUCH

Oval tinsel is a fine metallic chord that comes in a modest range of diameter. Wire is wire, and is now available in gold and silver and natural copper and all sorts of non-metallic colors such as olive and black and brown, in several diameters. Both tinsels and wires are used mainly to (1) add brightness to a fly; (2) suggest segmentation (as with the Skip's Quivering Cray); (3) toughen part of a fly by reinforcing it in a spiral (ribs); and (4) bind a wing to a fly-body Matuka-style (as with the Hare Waterpup and Shineabou Sunfish).

Flat tinsel is just a slim ribbon that adds little in durability but does add flash and can suggest segmentation. It comes in different widths and normally in two colors: silver and gold.

Finally, there are the bright reflective strands, such as Krystal Flash and Flashabou, that are usually used as or in the wings of sinking flies (as with the Clouser Minnow) and the tails of sinking, diving, and floating bass flies (the Skip's Sputterface and Dave's Diving Frog).

THREADS

Such light trout-threads as 8/0 and 6/0 are seldom used in bass flies (though they can serve well in many pan-fish flies). A light

bass-fly thread is 3/0. It's a sound choice for most everything but flared hair. For flaring hair, size-A rod-winding thread has become the standard. Actually, I've been using size-D rod-winding thread for a long time—it's so strong that it allows me to really tighten down on hair.

Other good hair-flaring threads are Kevlar and flat-waxed nylon. New threads come and go, and some have real believers among bass-fly tiers. Tying thread is really a personal matter, so there's no wrong choice. I prefer that my thread's color match or compliment the color of the hair I'm flaring with it, but a lot of tiers use white thread for all their flared-hair work.

HAIRS FOR FLARING

By far the most common hair used in bass flies is deer; elk is second. Deer is generally softer than elk and a bit easier to handle. Elk hair is generally coarser than deer, and stiffer and tougher and thicker-shafted. Elk is the more stubbornly buoyant of the two. In truth, though, packed deer is as buoyant as it needs to be.

The surprising thing is that at the extremes—the finest softest elk and the thickest coarsest deer—there isn't much difference.

I'd suggest you tie your first flared-hair bass flies with deer. You can later experiment with elk. Eventually you may prefer elk for the largest flies, elk for everything, deer for everything, or you may use each as it suits your fancy.

I've left antelope hair for last because I have only modest experience with it. According to Steve Kennerk, president of the Rocky Mountain Dubbing Company, processing antelope hair in the usual fashion makes it brittle. But Steve says that the antelope from his company, even the dyed stuff, is tough enough for good flaring, and I agree. I have found antelope hair to be thick-shafted (like elk) and soft (like deer). You can forget antelope for stacked-hair applications—its tips are nearly always broken.

My favorite hair for flaring is coarse and spongy. Some tiers prefer fine or soft hair. Sponginess is the constant in good flaring hair. A look and a bit of squeezing should tell.

Chris Helm, who markets deer hair for fly tiers, prefers hair from a deer's sides and rump. But having side- or rump-hair is no guarantee that you have good flaring hair—the particular species of the deer, its range, and even the season of its kill affect its hair. Trust to sound advice, a quality source, or your eyes and hands to find good flaring hair.

My favorite flaring hair is called "deer belly hair," whose source seems apparent. Naturally white, it comes in many dyed colors. The brightest colors of dyed deer, in fact, come from hair that starts out white. Sometimes bright is best, sometimes somber is best. It all depends upon the particular fly pattern, your personal taste, what you feel your bass prefer, and whether or not you are trying to imitate something.

OTHER HAIRS

Once it got out that sheep's wool could be flared and trimmed like deer hair, the race was on—bass flies (and flies for other fishes) began showing up with shaped-wool heads or bodies. Sure, wool isn't spongy and pocketed like the other flaring and shaping hairs we've explored, but it definitely can be made to flare and be trimmed to solid-looking shapes. Also like pocketed hair, I've discovered, it's quite buoyant.

That, in my experience, covers it regarding hair for flaring. But there are other kinds of hairs that find service in bass and pan-fish flies for purposes other than flaring. Here is a partial list:
• Buck tail (for wings and tails and such)
• Squirrel tail (gray or red-fox, wings, tails)
• Elk hair (wings, tails…)
• Calf tail (wings and tails again)

FEATHERS

"Hackles" are feathers from the neck or rump of a bird, usually a chicken hen or rooster. On trout flies, hackles are usually wound on the hook's shank, and while they can be wound for bass flies they are more often used to make wings for streamers or tails for both sinking and floating flies. A variety of hackles make good bass-fly tails, including big dry-fly neck hackles; "soft hackle," a broad, supple, thick-fibered rooster hackle; and hen back for smaller flies. My all-around favorite for bass-bug tails is rooster neck-hackle, the kind marketed specifically for streamers and bass flies. "Grizzly" hackles, white with black railroad-tie stripes crossways along their length, in both dyed and natural, seem particularly right in flies for both largemouth and smallmouth bass.

"Marabou" is a fluffy and ultra-soft feather that comes as plumes in many dyed colors. Marabou is so lively in water that it's popular in all sorts of flies, bass flies included. Only rabbit fur billows and pulses like marabou, but lacks marabou's versatile and considerable length.

The herls, peacock and ostrich, are flat plumes whose fibers are sort of slender feathers themselves—each is a stout quill thickly fringed. Peacock is the iridescent one, while ostrich is the softer of the two, with the longer (though still short) fringe. Both herls are common in trout flies, but both are used in bass-fly wings and tails.

Such popular trout-fly feathers as duck and turkey primaries and the many flank and breast feathers of guinea hen and partridge are seldom found in bass and pan-fish flies.

FURS

The hot fur right now for bass flies is rabbit, on the hide. The hide and fur are both supple and create a wing or tail that snakes and swells in sinking, diving, and even floating flies. Such hide-fur strips are called Zonker strips or just rabbit strips. If the fur slopes across the strip

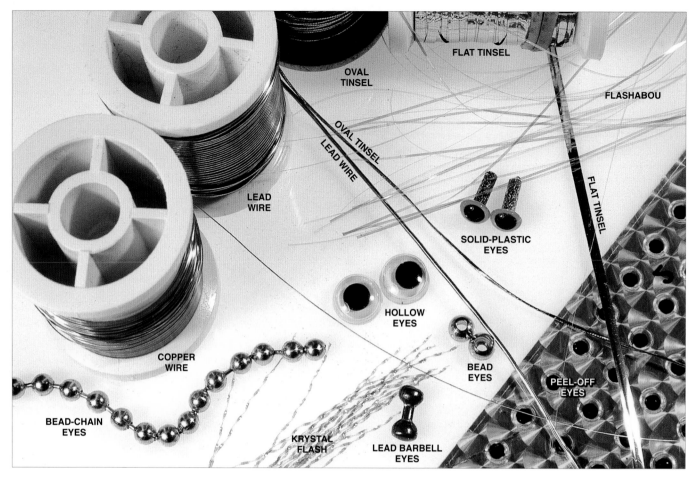

it's called a crosscut rabbit strip, made not for tails or wings but for winding up a hook's shank. Zonker and crosscut strips come in many dyed colors, some even barred. Fur-and-hide strips are also made from squirrel.

Rabbit and other furs, such as muskrat, squirrel, and synthetic dubbings such as Antron, are often "dubbed," spun onto thread, and wound for bodies or heads. Dubbed fur isn't used nearly so often in bass flies as it is in trout flies.

VARIOUS MATERIALS

These are the materials which seem to fit no category other than their own. Rubber-strand has long been popular for bass and pan-fish flies. It now comes in many colors and—at last!—in several thicknesses. The thicker strands usually go best with the largest flies and the thinner strands with the smaller flies.

Uses for all the standard synthetic eyes are demonstrated throughout this book, especially in section IV, "More Techniques." There are plastic eyes peeled from a sheet and backed with adhesive; plastic barbell eyes (shaped as their name suggests); solid-plastic eyes (some on a post you must cut off); clear, hollow eyes with lively, free pupils; bead-chain eyes (which come connected; you just snip off the beads in pairs); and lead (and lead-substitute) barbell eyes.

Supple, sparkling synthetic materials such as Antron and Mylar are blended with fur dubbing. The stouter Antron comes as a loose yarn. Sometimes the sparkle these materials provide suggests some aspect of the creature the fly imitates, but more often it's added simply to catch a fish's attention.

Foam is very buoyant and fairly tough. It's used in all sorts of ways and shows up in all sorts of flies, including bass and pan-fish flies.

Icelandic sheep hair is long, supple, and full and consequently shows up in some bass-fly wings.

Gelatinous-looking strand materials such as V-rib and D-rib are common in artificial nymphs, but only occasionally in bass flies.

In big trout flies, yarns—such as wool or Antron or Poly yarn—build fast when wound up a hook's shank to provide the kind of bulk that fills out a plump imitation stonefly nymph. But the bulk of yarn is almost insignificant when it comes to fat, three-inch long bass flies. Yarn is consequently seldom used in flies for bass.

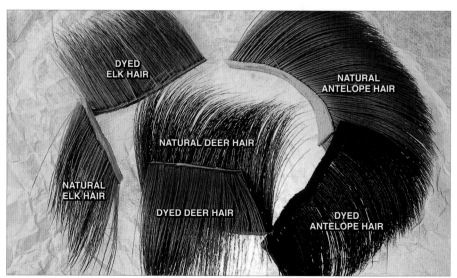

Elk, deer, and antelope hair—they may look similar, but you'll discover some significant differences when you tie with them. Note the ragged, broken tips of the antelope hair.

XI. Tools

Most fly-tying tools are the general kind used for tying all kinds of flies—trout flies, saltwater flies, steelhead flies, bass flies, whatever. Still, there are some fine points regarding tools as they apply to the tying of bass flies, and two tools—the hair packer and (although some would disagree) the half-hitch tool—are really much more about tying bass flies than flies of any other kind, at least in my experience.

Here, then, are fly-tying tools from the bass-fly tier's perspective.

VISE

A vise for all-around tying must be sturdy, hold a wide range of hooks securely, tighten and open easily, and allow plenty of tying access to the hook. A vise specifically for bass flies may not be required to hold small, fine hooks (unless that vise is also to be used for tying pan-fish flies), but it *really* needs an edge on holding big hooks securely. Some vises do all this—the trout flies, the bass flies, the works—through interchangeable jaws ranging from fine to stout and heavy duty.

I've come to prefer a "rotary" vise, one whose jaws indeed rotate, allowing me to comfortably work on the sides, top, or bottom of a fly. There are a few variations on the rotary style, and they all work and they all seem to have followers. Still, some fine tiers prefer a "stationary" vise, one with a set jaw position, and a good one can be had for significantly less cost than a comparable rotary vise.

Vises either mount in a C-clamp (which, in turn, mounts to a table), or mount in a "pedestal," a heavy, portable base. The C-clamp is the more secure, the pedestal is the more convenient. If you plan to tie always in the same place, the clamp makes sense. I tie in places from familiar to foreign, so the pedestal is my only real choice, but I'd probably choose it regardless.

SCISSORS

Get good scissors—ones that cut smoothly and consistently, ones that are made and marketed specifically for tying flies. Scissors aren't costly, so get a high grade. I like the ones with fine, nearly invisible, serrations that tend to grip whatever material I'm cutting. Your first scissors should have straight blades—and not the ultra skinny type made especially for fine work with small flies. Later, you can try scissors with curved blades if you like. Curved-blade scissors can be helpful in shaping flared hair, and for a few other tasks.

BOBBIN

A bobbin holds and feeds thread, and its hanging weight keeps tension on the thread to free the tier's hands. You need at least one bobbin. A good bobbin feeds thread smoothly, holds the thread-spool securely, and has a tube with a glassy inner surface that will not fray thread. I now prefer bobbins wide-diameter tubes for all my tying—easy to thread and unlikely to clog with the wax from pre-waxed thread.

HALF-HITCH TOOL

A half-hitch tool is a tapered metal rod with a hole at the small end of the taper. The hole goes over the hook's eye and the half hitch slides down the taper onto the shank. For years I treated the half-hitch tool as a gimmick, but I've since found it an indispensible aid in tying with flared hair (see "Spinning Hair" in section III, "Flaring and Shaping Hair").

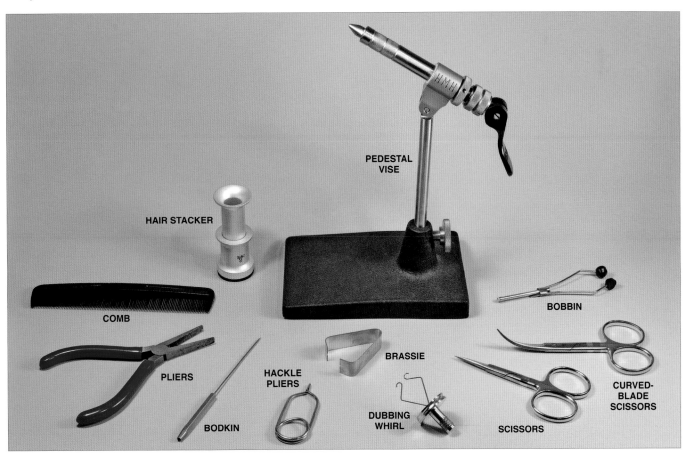

COMB

HAIR STACKER

PEDESTAL VISE

BOBBIN

PLIERS

BODKIN

HACKLE PLIERS

BRASSIE

DUBBING WHIRL

SCISSORS

CURVED-BLADE SCISSORS

HAIR PACKER

I've also seen this tool called a "hair compacter" and "hair compressor." Flaring hair is incidental in most fly tying, making the hair packer handy but hardly required—your thumb and finger can do the same work. The tying of bass flies, however, is truly an exercise in flaring and compressing hair, making the hair packer invaluable. Your thumb and fingers won't last long under the strain of compressing the hair on a dozen big Messinger Bucktail Frogs.

Some hair packers are simply a tube, sometimes with some kind of brace for applying pressure. I prefer a hair packer that primarily pushes on the thread-turns at the base of the hair, like the packer called the Brassie.

HAIR STACKER

The hair stacker consists of a flared tube and a removable end cap. I prefer a large-diameter stacker for all my tying. The hair is loaded tips-first into the stacker, the stacker is tapped against a firm surface, the stacker's cap is removed, and the hairs are removed with their tips evened. Flared-hair bass flies often include a skirt or collar of evened hair-tips, and then there are the occasional hair wings and tails—all of these call for the stacker. I could tie bass and pan-fish flies without a hair stacker, but I'd rather not.

LIGHT

You'll need generous light shining down onto the jaws of your vise if you want to tie presentable flies, and that goes for any kind of tying—trout, bass, whatever. The adjustable-arm desk-lamp remains the standard. Ambient light from a window or overhead light also helps.

That covers the tools I all but require on my bench when tying bass flies.

OPTIONAL TOOLS

You probably won't need any of these tools in order to tie bass and pan-fish flies, but some of them can make the task more pleasant and some are just fun.

MAGNIFIER

A magnifier is an optional aid for most tiers, but a godsend for the tier whose eyesight needs a boost. But that's just the mechanical angle. Fly tying is visual—seeing the process more clearly can only make it richer, more rewarding. So if tying is easier and more fun with magnification…well, why not?

I find magnification of around 3.0 about right for most tiers, but there's higher magnification if you need it. Reading glasses are a sound choice, and there are several magnifying systems made especially for fly tying. Currently my favorite magnifier—for when I'm serious about precision—is a "binocular magnifier," a hinged visor on an adjustable headband; the visor holds two lenses formed in one rectangle called a "lens plate." Binocular magnifiers are comfortable, their hinged visor is very handy, and they even fit over conventional glasses. You can purchase binocular magnifiers at jewelers' supply houses and at some fly shops.

Two magnifiers: reading glasses inside a binocular magnifier.

PLIERS

The main purpose of pliers in fly tying is to bend down hook-barbs to protect fish, but I do find other uses for them. I prefer pliers with small jaws whose inside surfaces are flat and smooth. Most fly shops carry such pliers.

BODKIN

A bodkin is just a handle with a needle. Bodkins are handy for a variety of tying tasks.

BLENDER

Commonly known as a coffee grinder, the blender is for quickly and thoroughly mixing two or more colors or types of dubbing. If a blender is run long, it will tend to chop fur. Sometimes chopped fur is best; if not, blend briefly. Blenders are great for natural dubbings, but I've had inconsistent results with synthetic dubbings. Common as they are in trout flies, dubbings of any kind are only incidental in tying bass flies, making a blender a luxury for a bass-fly specialist. That's especially true in light of the fact that you can blend dubbings by pinching clumps of them together in one hand and then pulling the resulting single clump in half with the other, and continuing this sequence until the two are well mixed. Hand blending is easier and quicker than it sounds.

Blenders can be found in fly shops, and in the kitchens of coffee enthusiasts.

DUBBING TWISTER

Dubbing twisters come in various forms, usually a hook at the end of a handle. A dubbing twister is used to twist a dubbing- or hair-filled loop of thread into a furry rope. A dubbing whirl is heavy and balanced and does its work in a free-spinning blur—it's fast, and I get a kick out of using it.

OLD SCISSORS

Old scissors—or cheap scissors or fingernail clippers—are useful for cutting hard things that might damage your sharp and at least slightly expensive working scissors—such things as wire, lead, and thick snag-guard monofilament. Deep inside the blades of any scissors can do this work, but with old scissors you can cut close, even with the points, which is sometimes just right. Never cut hard materials with the tips of good scissors—and never mix up your old scissors you saved for cutting wire with your crisp new scissors with their fine sharp points. Fingernail clippers are always an option…

MATERIAL HOLDER

A material holder is usually a spring or clip that holds materials back out of your way as you work. I'd hate to tie without one. I prefer the spring—it allows me to remove materials in any order since it has several slots.

WHIP FINISHER

The whip finisher helps the tier execute a standard finishing knot called a whip finish. I prefer to use my fingers, but some good tiers swear by whip finishers.

BOBBIN THREADER

I no longer use a bobbin threader. I prefer a loop of monofilament or a dental-floss threader. This is why I now use bobbins with wide-diameter tubes—they are nearly always easy to thread.

HACKLE GAUGE

Although a hackle gauge is truly a must for tying many trout flies—especially dry flies—it's only a maybe for tying bass flies. You could tie a lot of bass and pan-fish flies without missing a hackle gauge. But if you tie trout flies too… Besides, a few pan-fish flies do have conventional hackle collars for which the hackle gauge is a boon.

XII. BASS-FLY HOOKS

The established system for classifying a fly-hook's wire-thickness, shank-length, and size is confusing enough in general—but it's especially confusing when you try to apply it to the standard bass-fly hook. This standard bass-fly hook is often called a "stinger" hook. Its wire is stout, its bend varies, and its gape is a chasm. These elements are pretty consistent, although the stinger hook reforms itself slightly (sometimes considerably) as it passes through each manufacturer. Probably for these reasons this hook tends to defy the hook-classification system. Anyway, the result is that stinger-hook sizing gets crazy—look at the photo below and read the caption and you'll understand exactly what I mean.

So I used the system, very loosely, for describing the stinger hook's wire-thickness and gape in this book, but wound up describing its sizes through inches.

So why should the bass-fly tier bother with the standard fly-hook system at all? The best reason is that the system really does work well for almost all flies other than bass flies, and even at that, it does apply to bass flies that use one of those many hooks that's not a stinger. I guess I'd say simply, if you're going to tie, you need to understand the system. And I can make sense of it for you.

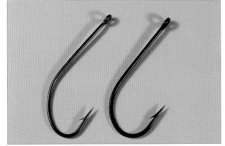

The size-10 Tiemco 8089 hook on the left is very nearly the same length as the Partridge size-2 CS41 hook on the right—a size-2 hook should be much larger than a size-10. Standard bass-fly hooks are so odd that fitting them to the established system for classifying a hook's shank-length, wire-thickness, and size is nearly useless.

SHANK LENGTH

A hook's shank (see the diagram on the right) can be "regular length," "short," or "long." A shank that is "regular length" or "standard length" is just that—that middle-of-the-road length by which long and short for a particular hook-size are judged.

Which brings us to the somewhat confusing "X"s. If a shank is slightly long, it is "1X long," slightly longer is "2X long," and a really long shank is "6X long." Same rules for short shanks—"1X short" is slightly short and "4X short" is very short. The eye and bend remain unchanged, regardless of shank length. There are formulas for determining *exactly* how shank-length "X"s work, but don't worry about them; for the most part, the hook manufacturers don't. My simple approach works fine.

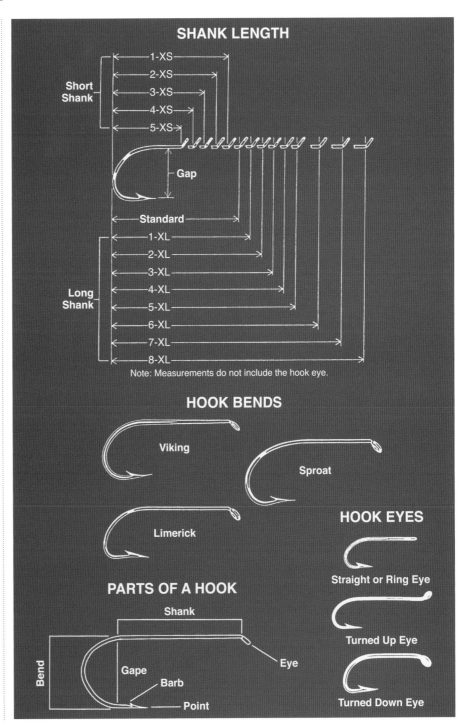

SHANK LENGTH

Short Shank
1-XS
2-XS
3-XS
4-XS
5-XS

Gap

Standard
1-XL
2-XL
3-XL
4-XL
Long Shank
5-XL
6-XL
7-XL
8-XL

Note: Measurements do not include the hook eye.

HOOK BENDS

Viking

Sproat

Limerick

PARTS OF A HOOK

Shank
Bend
Gape
Barb
Point
Eye

HOOK EYES

Straight or Ring Eye

Turned Up Eye

Turned Down Eye

Wire Thickness

The thickness of a hook's wire, like the length of its shank, is also gauged with an "X." Wire described as "regular" or "standard" is of a median thickness for a particular hook-size, the model by which other thicknesses are classified. If wire is one increment thicker than regular, it is "1X heavy," two increments thicker is "2X heavy," and so on. Same thing with fine wire—"1X fine (or '1X light')," "2X fine," and finer and finer.

Size

Hook-sizing can be confusing at first, but we all get used to it pretty quickly.

For size-1 and smaller, the system makes sense—the larger the number, the smaller the hook. So a size-2 hook is large, a size-8 is medium size, a size-14 is small, and a size-20 is tiny (too tiny for the tastes of bass and pan fish). Hooks larger than size-1 go by different rules—after size-1, an "/0" ("ought") follows the number; and the larger that number, the *larger* the hook. So a 2/0 hook is larger than a 1/0, and a 6/0 is much larger than either. The smaller, non-/0, hooks usually run only in even sizes. Here's a string of hook-sizes running from tiny to progressively larger: 18, 14, 12, 10, 8, 6, 4, 2, 1, 1/0, 2/0, 3/0, 4/0, 5/0, 6/0.

Get it?

Other Considerations

The eye of a fly hook can tip up, called an "up eye"; down, a "down eye"; or project straight off the shank, a "straight eye" or "ring eye." Most bass flies are tied on hooks with ring eyes, but there are plenty of exceptions. There seem to be no standards on eye-type for pan-fish flies, but in truth, eye-type is often really a matter of personal preference.

There are several designs of hook-bend (three standard ones are shown in the illustration on the previous page), and each has its believers and has proven itself over many years. Again, personal preference.

Selecting Hooks

Beyond all this, consider where you'll be fishing and what you'll be fishing for. Big largemouth bass can and do take little pan-fish flies on occasion—a light-wire hook in your Foam Spider may be fine for six-inch bluegill, but what if a three-pound bass winds up on that hook? Sure, you're not after bass, but you'd probably still want to land that unlikely three-pounder. So in this particular case, you'd probably go with a standard-wire hook, possibly even a heavy wire hook provided you tied the fly stout, with enough tying foam to hold that heavy hook up at the water's surface.

As far as specific hook brands and models go, you have a great deal to choose from these days. I suggest you hunt around on-line, ask a fly-fishing friend, talk to someone working in a fly shop, buy your hooks in small numbers, and then see if you like the hooks you chose after you've tied and fished with them. If I recommended specific hook designs and brands here, and you buy this book two years from now, some of the hooks I recommended might be gone… and better ones might be available.

If fly hooks are new to you, then *you* just got a wallop of information. Take it all in a bit at a time. You'll get it.

XIII. ADDITIONAL BASS AND PAN-FISH FLIES

FLOATING BASS FLIES

BASIC BASS BUG

Hook: Heavy wire, short shank, ring eye (bass-fly hook), any bass-fly size.
Thread: Usually, 3/0 for the tail, any hair-flaring thread for the body.
Snag Guard: Optional.
Tail: Hackles, rubber-strands, marabou, bright synthetic strands, buck tail, whatever.
Skirt or Collar: Usually, stacked deer-hair tips or hackles wound up the hook's shank. Optional.
Body: Flared hair (deer, elk...), tapered from smaller at the rear to larger in front, usually with a white face.
Legs: Rubber-strands (optional).
Comments: All those new variations on the basic bass bug that continually parade through the pages of the magazines and the vises of fly tiers have two things in common: a tail and a plump body. Without these two elements, they might be bass *flies*, but they wouldn't really be bass *bugs*. A few bass bugs, such as the Tap's Bug, have stayed around long enough to earn an identity and a name, but most come nameless and go the same way. So make up your own variations, fish them well, and they'll almost certainly work.

GRINNEL FLY
Jack Ellis

Hook: Heavy wire, short shank (bass-bug hook), a total hook-length of 3/4 to 1 1/4 inches.
Thread: Black 3/0 (I prefer size-A rod-thread for flaring the hair).
Snag Guard: Optional.
Tail: Natural rabbit fur on the hide, a 1/8-inch-wide strip about 4 inches long.
Collar: The stacked hair-tips from the head; the tips should reach slightly beyond the far edge of the bend.
Head: Flared natural deer hair, trimmed to a cone shape.
Eyes: For a floating fly, hollow plastic eyes with free pupils; for a sinking fly, solid plastic eyes. Eyes should be yellow with black pupils.
Comments: Jack Ellis describes this snake-imitation as "the most effective fly in my arsenal." Floating, it

suggests a snake that swims along the surface. Fished on a sinking or sink-tip line, it imitates a true water snake, one that lives much of its life under water.

SHEEP WAKER, SHAD
Dave Whitlock

Hook: Heavy wire, short shank, ring eye (bass-fly hook); Dave did not include sizes, but obviously it should be the size of a small shad.
Thread: For the wing: white 3/0. For the head: white hair-flaring thread.
Throat: Red SLF and red Antron mixed.
Wing: Light-green Krystal Flash over gray Icelandic sheep over yellow Icelandic sheep over yellow or clear Krystal Flash over white Icelandic sheep.
Lateral Line: Two strips of pearl Krystal Flash or Mylar tinsel, one on the outside of each wing. Outside the Mylar, one badger hackle on each side.
Head: Flared hair, gray bars over yellow on top, white for the underside.
Eyes: Solid plastic, yellow with black pupils.
Comments: The Sheep Waker, Shad is only one of several Sheep Waker variations that imitate specific fishes. Here are a few of those fishes: alewife, crappie, chub, shiner, smelt, dace. Dave fishes his Sheep Wakers either as true surface flies or as divers, I assume, on a sink-tip line.

STEWART'S DYING SIDEWINDER SHINER
Jim Stewart

Hook: Heavy wire, short shank, ring eye (bass-bug hook), a total hook-length of about 1 1/4 to 1 3/4 inches.
Thread: For the tail and snag guard: 3/0 (I use white). For the body: any hair-flaring thread (red or white).
Snag Guard: Optional.
Tail: Short orange marabou, over which are four white schlappen feathers (2 to 2 1/2 times the length of the shank), over which are two fairly short grizzly hackles.
Skirt: Long natural-gray deer, stacked, followed by short white deer, also stacked. I keep the butts short on all this hair, and flare the body-hair over those butts.
Body: White flaring hair with natural-gray bars down the back. Near the front, one bunch of red or orange deer beneath the white. Trim the body as shown

here from the underside—thin top and bottom, wide on the sides.
Eyes: Hollow plastic with free pupils; the eyes should be yellow with black pupils.
Comments: This fly suggests a shiner that is injured, floating on its side. Jim works it around schools of shiners under attack by largemouth bass. He also ties his Stewart's Dying Sidewinder to imitate a bluegill and a shad.

TAP'S BUG
Tap Tapply

Hook: Heavy wire, short shank, ring eye (bass-bug hook). I've never seen a hook-size range with this pattern, but it's probably standard.
Thread: Any hair-flaring thread in yellow or orange.
Snag Guard: Optional.
Tail: Orange buck tail. (Tap liked to bind buck hair with spongy butts for the tail, so those butts flared and blended with the body.)
Body: Orange deer at the bend, a band of black deer, and the front is yellow. Trim the body as shown in the photograph—basic bass-bug shape.
Comments: Tap Tapply was editor of *Outdoor Life* magazine when he created the Tap's Bug sometime in the 1940s. His bright-but-simple fly still gets talked about and fished—and it still catches plenty of smallmouth and largemouth.

WHITLOCK MOUSERAT
Dave Whitlock

Hook: Heavy wire, short shank, ring eye (standard bass-bug hook), a total hook-length of 1 1/4 to 1 3/4 inches.
Thread: Any pale hair-flaring thread (use 3/0 for binding on the tail if you like).
Snag Guard: Optional.
Tail: Chamois or rabbit hide with fur, trimmed to a long slender taper, about two full hook-lengths.
Body: Underside: pale natural deer hair. Top: stacked dark deer hair, butts trimmed short. Dave recommends roe deer or short shoulder-hair from a white-tailed deer for the top of the body.
Eyes: Black solid plastic.
Whiskers: Black squirrel tail, bear hair, or moose hair, bound on at the hook's eye.
Comments: Dave says he created his Whitlock Mouserat "in an attempt to make a more realistic mouse and baby muskrat imitation, lemming or vole."

WIGGLE-LEGS FROG
Dave Whitlock

Hook: Heavy wire, short shank, ring eye (bass-bug hook), a total hook-length of about 1 to 1 3/4 inches.
Thread: Any white or yellow hair-flaring thread.
Snag Guard: Optional.
Rump: Flared hair—olive over yellow over white.
Hind Legs: Each leg is green buck tail over white, bound around a ring-eye hook, pulled back and secured with thread-turns. The bend is then cut from the hook. Each leg is held loosely by a twisted-wire or monofilament loop which, in turn, is bound to the main hook.
Body: Flared hair, originally, olive over yellow over white, but now it's often tied with all kinds of color combinations over a white belly.
Front Legs: Three white rubber-strands, knotted and spread at the tips to suggest flippers.
Eyes: White with black pupils, solid or hollow.
Comments: This pattern comes from *The Fly Tyer's Almanac* by Robert Boyle and Dave Whitlock. The Wiggle-Legs Frog is a proven standard with a track record spanning more than three decades.

SINKING BASS FLIES

DAVE'S EELWORM STREAMER
Dave Whitlock

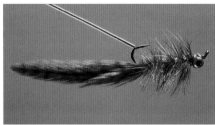

Hook: Heavy wire, 2X or 3X long, down eye, sizes 8 to 1/0.
Thread: Three-ought or heavier in a color similar to the body's color.
Tail: Four long, full hackles (rooster hackles, often called "bass hackles" or such, are ideal) in two sets, the sets cupping together. The tail can be up to twice the full length of the hook. Add a shorter hackle, flaring outward, on each side of the long hackles.
Eyes: Lead or lead-substitute barbell eyes, mounted atop the shank just behind the hook's eye. The eyes can be plain metal or painted.
Rib: Small- to medium-diameter copper wire.
Body: Dubbing (rabbit, Antron, Arizona Sparkle Nymph—dull, sparkling, shaggy, whatever you like). Standard colors are black, blue, purple, brown, wine-red, and green, but try yellow or white some time.
Hackle: One long and long-fibered, usually in the body's color (though not necessarily). "Bass hackle" rooster hackle does a fine job. Bind the hackle on right behind the eyes, spiral it back over the body, bind it with the rib and then spiral the rib forward through the hackle and over the body.
Head: The same dubbing as in the body, built up between the eyes.

Comments: I've modified the Dave's Eelworm Streamer slightly from the original Dave presents in *Fly-Tyer's Almanac*, published in 1975—mainly, I counter-ribbed the hackle for toughness and mounted the heavy eyes atop the shank to flip the fly upside down.

This has been a real standby for me for largemouth for a long time. Should be equally effective on smallmouth but I haven't shown it to them enough times to say.

FOAMTAIL SUPER WORM, PURPLE
Pat Ehlers

Hook: Jig hook (Pat prefers the "G-lock Worm Hook" shown here), size 3/0 (I sometimes tie it on smaller hooks).
Thread: Purple 3/0 or the like.
Snag Guard: Optional.
Eyes: Large red barbell lead or lead-substitute eyes, bound in the kink in the hook's shank.
Tail: Purple magnum (extra-wide) Zonker strip, about twice the full length of the hook. Bind the strip upside down (fur side against the hook) down the top of the shank.
Body: Polar Chenille in "UV Purple" wound with a purple cross-cut rabbit strip.
Wing: Purple Holographic Flashabou, bound just behind the eyes to lie back along each side of the body. About six purple or barred-purple rubber-strands bound atop the hook just behind the eyes. Trim both the Flashabou and the rubber-strand to about equal the length of the tail.
Foam Tail-Tab: Chartreuse 1/8-inch Evasote foam sheeting cut to about the width of the tail's hide and about twice as long as the tail is wide. Glue the foam-tab to the tip of the tail against the hide (Pat glues it with Zap Goo).
Comments: Pat's Foamtail Superworm is primarily for largemouth bass when it carries a snag-guard. Without the snag-guard it's equally a largemouth and smallmouth fly. He likes to either bounce it along the bottom of a river or lake with its tail high and wagging or just swim it back like a streamer. This one's really caught on.

HALF AND HALF
Lefty Kreh and Bob Clouser

Hook: Heavy wire, 3X long, up eye, sizes 6 to 2.
Thread: Three-ought in a color to match the wing.
Eyes: Lead barbell eyes painted red with black pupils.
Tail: Eight long saddle hackles divided into two sets and mounted with the sets cupped together. Outside this, a few strands of Krystal Flash and Flashabou. All this goes atop a small bunch of long buck tail. The buck tail should start at the hook's eye, hump bare and tight over the lead eyes' stem (as with a Clouser Deep Minnow), and should be lashed down the shank to the bend.
Wing: Two bunches of buck tail, the light color beneath; the dark on top. The darker color should match the thread. (By "on top" I mean with the hook inverted, as it will ride in the water.)
Comments: The Half and Half is the result of combining Lefty's Deceiver with the Clouser Deep Minnow. Tie it in any colors you wish. (You'll find tying instructions for the Half and Half in *Morris on Tying Flies.*

LEFTY'S DECEIVER, BLACK
Lefty Kreh

Hook: Heavy wire, short shank, ring eye (bass-bug hook), a total hook-length of about 1 to 1 3/4 inches.
Thread: Black 3/0.
Tail: Two sets of three to five black saddle hackles (I have seen the hackle-sets mounted both curving together and curving apart). Outside the hackles, six to ten strands of purple Flashabou. The hackles should be long and the Flashabou slightly longer.
Cheeks: A bunch of black buck tail on each side, extending beyond the far edge of the hook's bend.
Wing: Long black buck tail.
Beard: Red Krystal Flash, cut just short of the hook's point.
Eyes: Bright peel-off adhesive eyes under a layer of epoxy glue.
Comments: The Lefty's Deceiver is a longtime favorite among saltwater anglers, but this version Lefty designed specifically for largemouth bass. He says it is particularly effective in colored water. It's become very popular in some areas.

MEAT WHISTLE, RUST
John Barr

Hook: Heavy wire jig hook, sizes 3/0 to 1/0 (I tie it smaller as well).
Thread: Rust-brown 3/0 or 140-denier Ultra Thread.
Head: Copper metal conehead, for 3/0 hooks, large; for 2/0, medium; for 1/0, small. The cone stops against a cemented ball of thread at the hook's kink.
Rib: Copper-brown Ultra Wire, brassie (medium/small) size. Wind the rib up the body and the Zonker strip, Matuka-style.
Body: Copper Diamond Braid.
Wing: Rust Zonker strip.
Legs: Pumpkin Barred Sili Legs (or any pumpkin or orange-brown rubber strand), bound on just behind the conehead. Two legs on each side.
Collar: Copper Flashabou under brown marabou.
Collar (behind the metal cone): Rust rabbit dubbing.
Comments: John considers his rust version an imitation of a crayfish and, secondarily, a spiny little fish called a sculpin, for both smallmouth and largemouth bass. He fishes it in lakes, letting the fly sink below a floating line, and then swimming it or hopping or dragging it back along the bottom. But it's become a standard fly for smallmouth in rivers too. John also ties his Meat Whistle in olive and in black.

MORRIS MINNOW, CONEHEAD, SMALLMOUTH
Skip Morris

Hook: Heavy wire, short shank, straight eye (standard bass-bug hook), a total hook-length of about 1 to 1 3/4 inches.
Cone: Metal, brass or gold color.
Thread: Olive 6/0 or 3/0.
Body: Fine pearl Mylar strands (Angel Hair, Lite Brite…) for the underside, fine pale-yellow or gold mixed with olive strands along the sides, fine olive-brown or dark-olive strands on top. Build the body in three (or four) sections of Mylar, and then trim it to shape after the fly is tied.
Head: A short section of copper or gold woven Mylar tubing bound on at the rear of the cone and doubled back, inside out. Coat the tubing with epoxy glue back to the rear of the head-area, trim

the head to length (after the epoxy is almost set), paint the head with poster paints or watercolors or such (white underside, sides bare Mylar, top dark-olive, eyes red with black pupils, any other details you like), and add a final coat of epoxy glue.
Comments: Imitates a baby smallmouth bass, for catching adult smallmouth. There's a largemouth version too. On the mono loop knot, this fly shimmies its heart out. The uncommonly bright Morris Minnows have taken me many bass, trout, and other species, among them many of the biggest I've caught. (You'll find detailed tying instructions in *Fly Tying Made Clear and Simple II, Advanced Techniques*.)

SHENK'S WHITE STREAMER
Ed Shenk

Hook: Heavy wire, 3X or 4X long, sizes 10 to 2.
Thread: Black or gray 8/0, 6/0, or 3/0.
Tail: One white marabou plume, slightly shorter than the hook's shank.
Body: Cream or white fox fur wound in a dubbing loop and trimmed to minnow-shape (many tiers use rabbit fur).
Comments: In *Fly Fishing for Smallmouth Bass*, author Harry Murray says, "Shenk's White Streamer might just be my overall favorite streamer; it is definitely the best chub imitation I've found." Enough said?

SILVER OUTCAST
Charles Waterman

Hook: Heavy wire, short shank, ring eye (standard bass-bug hook), standard bass-streamer size range. (In his book *Black Bass and the Fly Rod*, Waterman describes all the materials but hook and thread. I made my best guesses from the illustration of the Silver Outcast in that book. Hook design and size and thread type and color aren't very important here, which may be why Waterman ignored them in his book.)
Thread: Black.
Body: Flat silver Mylar tinsel.
Wing: Peacock herl over blue buck tail over yellow buck tail over white. Waterman prefers the wing "pretty skimpy."
Comments: Waterman claims to have discovered and modified the Silver Outcast rather than having created it. It's long been a standard for largemouth bass.

DIVERS

DAHLBERG DIVER (ORIGINAL)
Larry Dahlberg

Hook: Heavy wire, short shank (bass-bug hook), the normal range of bass-fly sizes.
Thread: Three-ought for the tail, hair-flaring thread for the collar and body.
Snag Guard: Optional.
Tail: About 50 strands of gold Flashabou trimmed to about three full hook-lengths. Over the Flashabou, white marabou; over the white, brown marabou.
Collar and Body: Natural-dark deer hair.
Comments: Larry's original version. It's a proven taker of largemouth and smallmouth. It's just a little…scary.

MORRISFOAM DIVER
Skip Morris

Hook: Heavy wire, short shank (bass-bug hook), a total hook-length of about 1 to 1 3/4 inches.
Thread: Three-ought in a color to match the color of the foam.
Snag Guard: Optional.
Tail: A long triangle of rabbit hide with fur. The hide should be bound by its point with the fur down; the fur should slope away from the hide's point.
Body and Collar: Closed-cell soft foam-sheeting cut to the shape of a large triangle connected to a small triangle by a short, slim strip. The small triangle is bound at the bend, the slim strip is bound along the shank, and the large triangle is folded back and bound at the bend with a thread-collar. The triangles are then trimmed to a collar.
Legs: Rubber-strands bound outside the foam at the hook's bend (see "The Skip's Hover Bug." Legs are optional).
Comments: This was the precursor of the Skip's Fusion Bug; it's still a good choice. Try winding thick lead wire over the front half of the shank before tying the fly to make it really dive.

STEWART'S BASS-A-ROO
Jim Stewart

Hook: Heavy wire, short shank (bass-fly hook), a total hook-length of about 1 to 1 3/4 inches.
Thread: Orange 3/0 for the tail, yellow hair-flaring thread for the body.
Snag Guard: Optional.
Butt: Flourescent-orange chenille.
Tail: Yellow buck tail over orange buck tail; over the buck tail, gold Flashabou and pearlescent Krystal Flash; outside all this, dyed-yellow grizzly hackles, splayed; outside the hackles, red or orange marabou.
Skirt: Stacked yellow deer-hair tips.
Body: Yellow deer hair with a spot of brown hair inside gray atop the front half of the body. The hair is trimmed flat beneath; rounded along the length of the top; tapered along the sides and top of the body, about one half to two thirds back from the hook's eye.
Eyes: Solid-plastic, yellow with black pupils.
Comments: Jim looks for the dark spot atop the body after the Stewart's Bass-A-Roo is on the water—if the spot is up and showing, the fly has landed upright, but if only yellow shows, a tug or two will turn the fly upright.

TY'S TANTALIZER (IMPROVED)
Tim England

Hook: Heavy wire, short shank (bass-fly hook), the usual range of bass-fly sizes (I assume).
Thread: Yellow 3/0 for the tail; yellow or red hair-flaring thread for the collar and body.
Snag Guard: Optional.
Tail: Yellow marabou outside a few strands of pearl Krystal Flash; outside this, a cree hackle on each side.
Skirt: Black hair tips over brown tips over yellow tips; all tips evened.
Diving Collar: Black flared hair behind brown behind yellow. The collar should be perpendicular when viewed from the side, rounded when viewed from the front.
Head: Red flared hair. The head should be a flat plane with only a low angle on top, rounded beneath when viewed from the front. The underside should be trimmed well below the hook's shank.
Comments: Quite a different shape from the typical Dahlberg-style diving bass bug.

UMPQUA SWIMMING FROG
Dave Whitlock

Hook: Tiemco 8089, sizes 10 to 2.
Thread: Single-strand floss.
Snag Guard: Optional.
Tail: Pearl Krystal Flash inside three sets of hackles—dyed-olive grizzly outside dyed-olive or dyed-light-olive grizzly outside white. Under the hook, a short tuft of white marabou.
Skirt: Stacked olive-brown over black over yellow deer-hair tips.
Diving Collar: Olive deer hair.
Body: The top is olive-brown deer hair, with black stripes or top spots, with yellow along the sides; the underside is white. (A variation has a yellow belly and orange at the sides.) Trim the body with a short fringe along the lower edges.
Legs: Three sets of rubber strands, white, yellow, and black.
Eyes: Plastic eyes.
Comments: Similar to the Dahlberg Diver but with a fringe that creates a slightly different diving motion than the Dahlberg's.

INSECTS AND CRAYFISH

CLOUSER'S CRAYFISH
Bob Clouser

Hook: Heavy wire, 3X or 4X long, sizes 10 to 6.
Thread: Olive or green 8/0, 6/0, or 3/0.
Weight: Two strips of lead wire, each bound along one side of the hook's shank.
Nose-Antennae: A few pheasant-tail fibers under the tip of a hen-mallard flank-feather.
Back and Tail: Olive Furry Foam.
Claws: Two hen-mallard flank-feathers with stems partly stripped and centers snipped out.
Underside: Pale gray yarn or dubbing.
Legs: One ginger-grizzly hackle spiraled up the abdomen before the Furry Foam is folded forward from the bend.
Rib: Gray thread (I use size-A rod-winding thread). There should be four ribs; try to place them between the turns of hackle.
Comments: The whip finish that completes this fly is made at the hook's eye, over the base of the Furry Foam tail.

FOAM DAMSEL

Hook: Light wire, 1X long (dry-fly hook), sizes 14 and 12.
Thread: Blue or black 8/0 or 6/0.
Abdomen, Back, and Head: Cylindrical soft closed-cell foam, blue or marked to blue with a permanent marking pen. (A strip cut from foam-sheeting also works well.)
Wings: Grizzly hackle, wound on the hook's shank and then trimmed top and bottom.
Comments: There are times when both largemouth bass and bluegill will refuse all but a damsel adult. This one has served me honorably during those times.

FOAM DRAGONFLY
David Lucca

Hook: Heavy wire, short shank (a large, stout dry-fly hook or a small bass-bug hook).
Thread: Blue 8/0, 6/0, or 3/0.
Abdomen: Gray closed-cell foam-sheeting. The abdomen is formed by segmenting a strip of foam up a fine needle called a "beading needle"; the needle is locked in a tying vise. When the abdomen is completed, it is then slid off the needle.
Wings: Fine deer hair, split into two wings straight out to the sides. Over the wings, a few strands of clear Krystal Flash.
Thorax: Gray dubbing, over which is the foam-strip.
Head and Back: The same foam-strip used to make the abdomen is pulled over the back; bound down over the front of the hook's shank; and then folded back, bound, and trimmed for the head.
Eyes: Hollow plastic eyes with free pupils, glued to the sides of the head.
Comments: Another good adult-dragon imitation. I've taken a lot of largemouth on it.

GIRDLE BUG

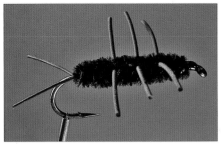

Hook: Heavy wire, 3X or 4X long, sizes 10 to 2.
Thread: Black 8/0, 6/0, or 3/0.
Tail: Two black rubber-strands.
Legs: Black rubber-strands, three sets.
Weight: Lead wire, wapped up the shank and around the strand-legs (weight is optional).
Body: Black chenille, fine or full, to suit either the hook-size or your preference.
Comments: Everything about this fly seems to be in question: whether the les are evenly distributed along the shank or bunched to the front, whether rubber-strand antennae should be added, how thick the chenille should be, who created the Girdle Bug, and even whether it really is a Girdle Bug! My limited research indicates that with black legs it is the Girdle Bug and with white legs it is the Rubber Legs, but you'll see this reversed in some books and articles. However you refer to them, both the Girdle Bug and Rubber Legs are great for both smallmouth bass and trout.

HOLSCHLAG
HiTAIL CRAW, NATURAL
Tim Holschlag

Hook: Heavy wire, 1X to 4X long, down eye, size 4.
Thread: Brown 3/0 (Tim uses Danville size-A).
Weight: Lead barbell eyes, 1/40 to 1/60 ounce.
Butt: A strip of gray or brown 1/16-inch-thick foam-sheeting cut to a 5/16-inch-wide 3/4-inch-long pointed strip. Better to use too much foam rather than too little; you can always trim a little off on the water to get the fly's action right.
Claws: Rust (or substitute brown) Zonker strips. Total length of each claw from the base to the tip of the fur is one inch.
Rib: One ginger or light-brown saddle hackle.
Body: Medium-diameter rust (or brown) chenille.
Comments: Tim also ties a green version in size 2, with a 1/2-inch long 1/4-inch-diameter chartreuse foam dowel in place of the foam strip. The 1/40 to 1/60-ounce barbell eyes are panted orange, claws olive, hackle chartreuse, and chenille olive.

Tim fishes a HiTail Craw by letting it lie on the riverbed and sway with the current, head and claws raised in a real crayfish fight stance, for three to five seconds before giving the fly a hop. A small strike indicator up the leader tells with its twitches when a bass has taken the resting fly. Quite a concept.

MORRIS FOAM PREDATOR
Skip Morris

Hook: Heavy wire, 2X to 4X long, Sizes 12 to 4.
Thread: Brown 3/0.
Tail: Pheasant-tail fibers, short (optional).
Back: A strip of soft, brown closed-cell foam-sheeting, 1/8-inch thick and about half as wide as the hook's shank is long.
Belly: Cream-to-tan rabbit fur, dubbed up the rear two thirds of the hook's shank.
Head: A strip of soft, brown closed-cell foam, about 1/8-inch thick and about as wide as the hook's gape.
Eyes: Melted monofilament or premade plastic barbell eyes.
Wing Case: Completely optional, but if you want one, just trim the doubled-back head-strip of foam straight across, and then taper it back over the body with a razor blade.
Legs: Brown or black rubber-strand, one length bound on each side.
Comments: I developed the Morris Foam Predator for trout fly, and it's proved itself with them. When I finally gave it a chance with largemouth bass, it proved just as effective with them as it had with the trout. It's fished on a sinking line—the line finds the bottom while the fly (on an active retrieve) hovers just above lake-bed snags. The Morris Foam Predator has also taken me some big smallmouth in lakes.

MURRAY'S HELLGRAMMITE
Harry Murray

Hook: Heavy wire, 2X or 3X long, sizes 10 to 4.
Thread: Black 3/0.
Weight: Lead wire, about the diameter of the hook's shank, covering the middle three quarters of the shank.
Tail: About 20 dyed-black ostrich herls, their very tips pinched off. The tail should equal the hook's full length, or be slightly longer.
Antennae: Two fine, black rubber-strands.
Rib: A soft dark-blue-dun saddle hackle, wound up the full length of the body in four to six ribs.
Body: Black chenille, full.
Comments: Hellgrammites can be abundant in smallmouth-bass streams, and Murray's Hellgrammite is a widely trusted imitation.

SKIP'S DAD
Skip Morris

Hook: Light to heavy wire, standard length to 2X long, sizes 12 to 6.
Thread: Brown 8/0, 6/0, or 3/0.
Nose: The same dubbing used for the abdomen.
Weight: Lead or lead-substitute barbell eyes bound atop the shank at the hook's bend.
Claws, Back, and Tail: Pheasant-tail fibers, the tips split and bound into two shank-long claws, the center of the fibers pulled forward over the abdomen and bound in front and wound with the rib, the butts splayed and bound and trimmed over the hook's eye as the tail.
Thorax: Brown Antron dubbing (or another synthetic or natural dubbing).
Rib: Copper wire.
Abdomen: The same dubbing used for the thorax.
Comments: This is the crayfish imitation I talk about in the chapter titled "The Skip's Quivering Cray"—right time, right river, worked down on the bottom, it's deadly.

PAN-FISH FLIES

BUMBLE McDOUGAL
Jack Ellis

Hook: Heavy wire, 2X long, size 8.
Thread: Black 8/0 or 6/0 (I prefer a hair-flaring thread for the body).
Tail: Dyed-yellow buck tail, the darker center hairs.
Body: Alternating bands of black and yellow deer hair, plump.
Wings: Cree or grizzly hackle tips.
Hackle: Grizzly, cree, or one black and one yellow hackle mixed.
Comments: The heavy wire hook is meant to push the fly down into the surface, but a standard dry-fly hook works perfectly well if your bluegill aren't ultra picky. Obviously, the Bumble McDougal imitates a bumble bee. According to Jack, both honey bees and bumble bees are plentiful around the flowering water plants of his east Texas ponds and lakes each spring. The bees, he says, often end up in the water... and in the mouths of bluegill. The Bumble McDougal is part of Jack's Dixie McDougal series, which also includes a wasp and a mud dauber.

F-C MACKIE BUG, RED/BROWN
Theodore Mackie

Hook: Heavy wire, 3X long, size 10.
Thread: Red 6/0 (or 8/0).
Tail: The same rubber-strand used for the legs. Two tails, shank length.
Under-Body: Heavy thread (such as flat waxed nylon) or a fine yarn built up to a torpedo shape, to thicken the abdomen and thorax.
Rib: Gold flat (or oval) textured or "holographic" (or plain) tinsel, small.
Abdomen: Brown Antron dubbing.
Legs: Clear metal-flake (or white or about any color you like) medium-diameter flat (or round) rubber-strand. Four legs spread over the top half of the abdomen, reaching back only to the bend.
Thorax: Red Antron dubbing.
Comments: Brent Hinds ties the F-C Mackie Bug for Feather-Craft Fly Fishing and suggests fishing it just under the surface near cover (lily pads, reeds…) on a floating line for bluegill and other pan fishes. Swimming the fly slowly with twitches and pauses is the standard retrieve in my experience. Brent says he knows anglers who fish an F-C Mackie Bug on a sinking line in rivers for smallmouth. Bob Story, who owns and manages Feather-Craft, describes the F-C Mackie Bug as his company's "best bluegill bug" and says he catches "carp and 'surprise' largemouth on it all the time."

FENCE RIDER
Jack Ellis

Hook: Heavy wire, short shank (bass-bug hook) a total hook-length of about 7/8 of an inch. (Jack uses a Mustad 3366, size 6.)
Thread: Black 6/0 for the tail and snag guard; black 3/0 for flaring hair (I prefer a heavier thread for flaring the hair).
Snag Guard: The Ellis-style pan-fish snag guard (see "The Fathead Diver" in section IX, "Pan-Fish Flies").
Tail: Two cree or grizzly hackle tips, splayed, two

hook-shanks in length; inside the hackles, brown marabou, 1 1/2 shanks in length, over a shank-long tuft of fox squirrel tail (red-fox, I believe).
Skirt: Stacked olive deer-hair tips.
Body: Alternating bands of dyed-olive and natural-pale deer hair, shaped as a normal bass-bug body.
Eyes: Hollow plastic eyes with free pupils.
Comments: The most significant characteristic of the Fence Rider is its size—small enough to hook a big bluegill but large enough to interest a largemouth bass.

J'S GRINCHWORM
Jesse Riding

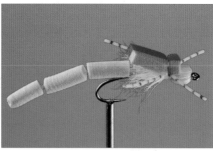

Hook: Fine or standard wire, 2X long, slow curve, sizes 14 to 10.
Thread: Chartreuse 8/0 or 6/0.
Abdomen: Chartreuse foam cylinder (some are marketed as posts for parachute hackles; others are marketed for damselfly bodies and such). You can color white foam with a marking pen. Short sections of the foam are strung along yellow 50-pound gel-spun fly-line backing, knotted behind each section, and glued with Zap-a-Gap or another cement. The sections are strung using a big sewing needle.
Head: Chartreuse deer hair doubled back as a bullet head.
Collar: The stacked tips of the head-hair. Trim off the hair-tips on the underside.
Legs: Fine barred chartreuse rubber-strand (or any fine, pale rubber strand).
Indicator: Red and orange strike indicator foam (or a rectangle of red or orange foam sheeting).
Comments: Jesse told me that he started out to develop an imitation of the inchworm for trout and wound up with an inchworm-like attractor fly for bluegill, crappie, yellow perch, and even smaller smallmouth bass. The jointed body shifts and bends in a living way whenever the fly is twitched on the water.

McGINTY

Hook: Heavy wire, standard length or 1X long, sizes 14 to 8.
Thread: Black 8/0 or 6/0.
Tail: Barred teal fibers over red hackle fibers.
Body: Yellow and black chenille wound together for a banded effect.
Hackle: Brown hen neck, angled back in traditional wet-fly style.

Wing: Blueish-black mallard wing quill with a white tip (or mark a white duck primary with a permanent marking pen).
Comments: The McGinty wet fly was, I believe, originally a trout fly, but it's long been a standard for pan fish. Obviously, it imitates a bee, and Jack Ellis says that when bees are on the water, a McGinty fished with only the tiniest quivers is deadly for bluegill—but the fly's probably been fished far more often for both trout and pan fish on a lively swimming retrieve (even though bees are horrid swimmers).

SILVER MINNOW (Brass Wonder)
Tim England

Hook: Heavy wire, 1X long, sizes 14 to 8.
Thread: Red 8/0 or 6/0.
Head: A nickle-plated brass bead.
Wing: White marabou over a few strands of pearl Krystal Flash over gray marabou, a few strands of peacock herl under the shank; each should be about two full hook-lengths.
Comments: Essentially a fast-sinking little streamer for all kinds of pan fish.

WOOLLY WORM

Hook: Heavy wire, 2X to 3X long, sizes 14 to 8.
Thread: Black 8/0 or 6/0 (or a color to match the color of the body).
Tail: Red hackle fibers.
Rib: One saddle hackle palmered up the body in six to nine ribs.
Body: Chenille.
Comments: Black and olive are likely the most common overall colors for the Woolly Worm, but anything goes. An old trout fly often used for pan fish. Charles Waterman, in his book *Black Bass and the Fly Rod*, speaks often of his faith in Woolly Worms for pan fish.

INDEX